I

Aristotle's *The Nicomachean Ethics*
(Books I–III, VI and X)

Already published in 'The SCM *Briefly* Series'

Anselm's *Proslogion*
Aquinas' *Summa Theologica Part I*
Aquinas' *Summa Theologica Part II*
Aristotle's *The Nicomachean Ethics*
Ayer's *Language, Truth and Logic*
Descartes' *Meditation on the First Philosophy*
Hume's *Dialogues Concerning Natural Religion*
Hume's *An Enquiry Concerning Human Understanding*
Kant's *Groundwork of the Metaphysics of Morals*
Kant's *Religion within the Boundaries of Mere Reason*
Kierkegaard's *Fear and Trembling*
Mill's *On Liberty*
Mill's *Utilitarianism*
Moore's *Principia Ethica*
Nietzsche's *Beyond Good and Evil*
Plato's *The Republic*
Russell's *The Problem of Philosophy*
Sartre's *Existentialism and Humanism*

Briefly:
Aristotle's *The Nicomachean Ethics*

(Books I–III, VI and X)

David Mills Daniel

scm press

© David Mills Daniel 2007

The Author has asserted his right under the Copyright, Designs and
Patents Act, 1988, to be identified as the Author of this Work

The author and publisher acknowledge material reproduced from
Aristotle, *The Nicomachean Ethics*, translated by J. A. K. Thomson
(Notes and Appendices by H. Tredinnick, Introduction and
Further Reading by J. Barnes), further revised edition, London:
Penguin Books, 2004. ISBN 0140449493.

British Library Cataloguing in Publication data

A catalogue record for this book is available
from the British Library

978 0 334 04131 3

First published in 2007 by SCM Press
9–17 St Alban's Place,
London N1 0NX

www.scm-canterburypress.co.uk

SCM Press is a division of
SCM-Canterbury Press Ltd

Typeset by Regent Typesetting, London
Printed and bound in Great Britain by
Bookmarque Ltd, Croydon, Surrey

Contents

Introduction

The SCM *Briefly* series, edited by David Mills Daniel, is designed to enable students and general readers to acquire knowledge and understanding of key texts in philosophy, philosophy of religion, theology and ethics. While the series will be especially helpful to those following university and A-level courses in philosophy, ethics and religious studies, it will in fact be of interest to anyone looking for a short guide to the ideas of a particular philosopher or theologian.

Each book in the series takes a piece of work by one philosopher and provides a summary of the original text, which adheres closely to it, and contains direct quotations from it, thus enabling the reader to follow each development in the philosopher's argument(s). Throughout the summary, there are page references to the original philosophical writing, so that the reader has ready access to the primary text. In the Introduction to each book, you will find details of the edition of the philosophical work referred to.

In *Briefly: Aristotle's The Nicomachean Ethics*, we refer to Aristotle, *The Nicomachean Ethics*, trans. J. A. K. Thomson (notes and appendices by H. Tredennick, Introduction and Further Reading by J. Barnes), further revised edition, London: Penguin Books, 1976, ISBN 0140449493.

Each *Briefly* begins with an Introduction, followed by a chapter on the Context in which the work was written. Who

was this writer? Why was this book written? With Some Issues
to Consider, and Some Suggestions for Further Reading, this
Briefly aims to get anyone started in their philosophical investigation. The Detailed Summary of the philosophical work
is followed by a concise chapter-by-chapter Overview and an
extensive Glossary of terms.

Bold type is used in the Detailed Summary and Overview
sections to indicate the first occurrence of words and phrases
that appear in the Glossary. The Glossary also contains
terms used elsewhere in this *Briefly* guide and other terms
that readers may encounter in their study of Aristotle's *The
Nicomachean Ethics*.

Traditionally, *The Nicomachean Ethics* and Aristotle's other
books are referenced by 'Bekker numbers'. Readers who want
more information about the Bekker numbers should refer
to the Penguin edition (Thomson, Tredennick and Barnes),
pages liii–iv.

Context

Who was Aristotle?

Aristotle, the son of Nicomachus, a court physician, was born in Stagira, in Macedonia, in 384 BC. At the age of 17, he went to Athens to study at Plato's Academy, where he stayed, as student and teacher, for 20 years. Plato's death in 347 BC led to changes at the Academy, and Aristotle moved first to Assos in Asia Minor, where he married Pythia, the niece of the ruler, Hermias, and then to Lesbos, before returning to Macedonia. In 343 BC, King Philip of Macedonia, who had established Macedonian supremacy over Greece, invited him to become tutor to his son, Alexander, the future Alexander the Great. In 335 BC, the year after Alexander succeeded Philip, Aristotle returned to Athens. He established his own school, the Lyceum, just outside the city, where he taught for the next 12 years, and established a large library of manuscripts and a museum of natural objects. It was also known as the Peripatetic School, due to Aristotle's practice of walking around as he talked with his students. After Alexander's death in Babylon, in 323, following his conquest of the Persian empire, Aristotle, fearing an anti-Macedonian reaction in Athens, left for Chalcis, where he died a year later.

Aristotle's interests went well beyond what are now regarded as philosophical subjects, and extended to science and natural history. He is believed to have written a large number of works, and although only a small fraction of these have survived, they show the enormous range of his interests. There are treatises on logic, including the *Categories* and *De Interpretatione*; metaphysics, *The Metaphysics*; ethics (see below) and politics, the *Politics*; physics, biology and psychology, including the *Physics*, the *Historia Animalium* and *De Anima*; and poetry and rhetoric, *Rhetoric* and *Poetics*. Although he spent many years as a student of Plato, he became a critic of Plato's philosophical ideas, including his theory of the forms (see below). His own approach to philosophy emphasized careful analysis of concepts and the importance of experience and observation. Aristotle's philosophical ideas had an immense influence on medieval thinkers, such as Thomas Aquinas, who refers to him as 'The Philosopher'.

What is *The Nicomachean Ethics*?

Aristotle's surviving works contain two books on ethics, *The Nicomachean Ethics*, probably edited by his son, Nicomachus (hence the title), and *The Eudemian Ethics*, probably edited by his pupil, Eudemus. Both books are based on notes for courses of lectures on ethics that Aristotle delivered at the Lyceum, which is why they contain inconsistencies and repetitions. *The Nicomachean Ethics* is the more important of the two, as it represents a later stage in the development of Aristotle's thinking on the subject. This *Briefly* covers five of the ten books of *The Nicomachean Ethics*: Book I ('The Object of Life'), Book II ('Moral Goodness'), Book III ('Moral Responsibility: Two Virtues'), Book VI ('Intellectual Virtues') and Book X ('Pleasure and the Life of Happiness').

What is The Nicomachean Ethics?

Aristotle had a teleological view of the world: everything has an end or purpose, which is determined by its nature or function. The (supreme or highest) good for all things, including human beings, is to fulfil this end or purpose, so it is both what they ought to aim at, and also what they actually do aim at; and the task of ethics is to identify the supreme or highest good for human beings. This (Book I) has an important bearing on how people lead their lives, as they are more likely to achieve their aim, if they have a definite target to aim at.

So what are the supreme end or purpose, and, thus, the supreme good, for human beings? Aristotle has no doubt that both ordinary and educated people agree that it is happiness (the Greek word *eudaimonia* means happiness or prosperity, which suggests well-being). This is because happiness is a final end, which is pursued for its own sake, not for the sake of something else (happiness is always a final end, never a means to anything else); is completely satisfying; and makes life desirable. But this raises further questions, because there are different views as to what constitutes human happiness, with the masses believing it is pleasure or money. Aristotle identifies three main types of life that are held to be happy: the pleasure-seeking or hedonistic life; one devoted to pursuit of political honours; and what he calls the 'contemplative' life: the life of the intellect, pursuit of philosophical truth and scientific knowledge. He dismisses the first kind of life as 'bovine', while wealth, a popular alternative to pleasure, is only a means to something else, not an end in itself. The problem with the political life is that political honours, unlike attainment of philosophical truth, depend, not on the individual himself, but on those from whom he receives them. This leaves the contemplative life (but Aristotle postpones detailed discussion of it).

3

In fact, to discover what constitutes happiness for human beings, we have to look at their nature and function to determine what sort of beings they are. And the distinctive feature of human beings, which separates them from other living things, is that they are rational. Thus, Aristotle concludes that human happiness is 'an activity of the soul', in accordance with 'a rational principle' and the 'best and most perfect kind of virtue'. However, this requires further explication, because, for Aristotle, 'virtue' does not have the primarily moral associations it now has; it is any kind of excellence. He explains that the human soul or personality is partly rational and partly irrational, and that the appetitive or desiring part of the latter, which may be classed as rational, along with the rational part proper, is, in self-controlled people, capable of obeying the latter, as a child does a parent. These two parts of the soul have their corresponding classes of virtues or excellences: the moral (those of character) and the intellectual, respectively. Human happiness consists in pursuing and practising these: although this does not tell us which kind of virtue is better.

Aristotle makes a number of other important points in Book I. We discover the good for human beings, and what they ought to aim at, by studying human beings and observing life, not in a transcendental or intelligible realm, set over against the empirical one, to which the philosopher must gain access, in order to acquire knowledge. Aristotle explicitly rejects Plato's theory of the forms, and the form of the good as the source of reality, truth and goodness. He links ethics to politics, which seeks to determine what we should and should not do in society, reflecting the fact that human beings do not lead their lives in isolation, but as members of communities. He acknowledges that both ethics and politics are not exact sciences: we must not look for more precision in these subjects than their nature permits. His concern is not with the ethical qualities of individual acts, but with development of the virtues that will enable people to lead good lives: the function of a good man is to lead his life well, and he will be happy throughout it, as he will spend it in virtuous conduct and contemplation, but it is only when his life is complete, and it is clear that this is how he has spent his life, that he can rightly be called happy. Popular belief, which holds that the happy man lives well, supports the philosophical analysis of happiness. Aristotle also notes that people need material goods to practise the moral virtues, as fine deeds cannot be performed without resources.

In Book II, Aristotle discusses the moral virtues. Like crafts, they are acquired by habit. In the same way that people become good builders by building well, they become just by performing just acts, so the habits we develop from the earliest age, through the actions we perform, play a vital part in determining our moral dispositions. We need to recognize that the actions which promote or destroy the moral virtues are of the same kind as those that flow from them: for example, we become temperate by refraining from, not indulging in, pleasures; and are best able to refrain from them when we are temperate. Aristotle stresses that it is impossible to give more than an outline account of right conduct, as we have to consider the circumstances of each situation, but there are some important points to bear in mind. Right conduct is incompatible with excess or deficiency in feelings or actions, which destroy our moral qualities, just as eating or drinking too much or too little destroys health. Our attitude towards pleasures and pains is an important indicator of our degree of moral goodness. Pleasures make us behave badly, and pains deter us from fine actions, while we can become bad through them by seeking or shunning the wrong ones. We need to develop the right attitude towards them, and educate ourselves to feel joy and grief at the right things. We must also appreciate that a virtuous act is not virtuous merely because it has a certain external quality, but only if the agent knows what he is doing; chooses to perform the action for its own sake; and does so from a permanent disposition: a person is just or temperate only if he performs an action in the way just or temperate people do.

Aristotle describes virtues as 'dispositions'. What does this mean? A disposition is not a feeling (like anger or fear), or a faculty (being capable of having such feelings), for neither of which people are called good or bad, or praised or blamed, but a condition of being well or ill-disposed towards something, and being inclined to act towards it in a particular way. Thus, our disposition towards anger is good if we have a moderate tendency towards it (and so do not become angry, except for good cause). As to the kind of disposition, a moral virtue is a human excellence, which, like any excellence, makes that of which it is an excellence good, and enables it to perform its function well: so, moral virtues are dispositions that make someone a good human being and enable him to perform his function well.

The moral virtues involve Aristotle's famous doctrine of the mean. He explains that something continuous and divisible (such as a length of wood) can be divided in a number of ways, including into two equal parts, which would be the mean (the half-way point) between the two extremes of excess and deficiency. This is an objective mean, as everybody would accept it is the halfway point between two parts, which would otherwise be unequal in length to varying degrees. However, there is also a relative mean. Six pounds is the objective mean

in relation to ten pounds of food, but a trainer would not necessarily give this amount to a particular athlete, as it might be
too much or too little for him. The mean here would be the appropriate amount for the particular athlete. It is this second,
relative mean that the moral virtues, which concern feelings
and actions, aim to hit. We can, and do, feel fear, anger, pleasure, and so on, too much or too little. The right way is to avoid
excess or deficiency, and have, or do, them to an intermediate
degree. This seems clear enough.

Aristotle has already said that right conduct is incompatible with excess or deficiency in feelings or actions, and the
doctrine of the mean seems to reinforce this point. However,
it will not always be easy to determine what the mean is. The
mean in relation to anger may not always be a moderate degree of anger. It will vary according to the situation, and in
some situations extreme anger will be appropriate. The doctrine of the mean does not provide a clear-cut rule, which can
be followed easily in every situation; it is a general guiding
principle. As Aristotle acknowledges, the mean is a difficult
target to hit.

He explains that the mean does not apply to feelings and
actions like malice and murder, which are evil in themselves,
and not through excess or deficiency, and shows how the doctrine of the mean applies to particular virtues. For example,
with fear and confidence, courage is the mean, rashness the
excess, and cowardice the deficiency, while, in relation to anger, the mean is patience, and the extremes irascibility and
lack of spirit. However (underlining its relative nature), the
mean is not in all cases equidistant between the extremes of
excess and deficiency. For example, the deficiency of cowardice is further from the mean of courage than the excess of
rashness. We also tend to view the (wrong) things towards

which we are more inclined as being more opposed to the mean.

Aristotle accepts that being morally virtuous and achieving the mean point in feelings and actions is difficult. For example, it is easy to get angry, but hard to feel or act towards the right person to the right extent, at the right time, for the right reason and in the right way. But there are rules we can follow, which will help us to hit the mean. We must try to avoid the extreme that is more contrary to the mean; recognize our individual weaknesses, and force ourselves in the opposite direction; and be vigilant about pleasures, as we do not judge them impartially.

Moral responsibility (Book III) raises the issue of voluntary and involuntary actions: we are held accountable, and praised or blamed, for the former, but not the latter, and, as moral agents, we need to understand the difference between them. Involuntary actions are those arising from external compulsion or ignorance, but the dividing-line between the two kinds of action is not absolutely clear-cut. There are mixed actions when, strictly, the agent has the power to perform, or not perform, the action, but is forced (as by threats to his family) into a wrong action, which, in normal circumstances, he would not choose to do. However, Aristotle does not think that such situations excuse any action the agent performs, however bad: there are some things people would, and should, rather die than do, and agents are blamed or praised according to the extent to which they have, or have not, yielded to compulsion. Further, the agent cannot blame external factors, if he succumbs to them easily, and cannot take credit for fine acts, but then try to avoid responsibility for disgraceful ones, by attributing them to the compulsive effects of pleasure.

Aristotle further maintains that it is only ignorance of

particular circumstances, as when the agent is mistaken
about what he is doing, not ignorance of a moral principle,
that makes an act involuntary; and someone who performs a
wrong act, due to the first kind of ignorance, should feel pain,
and show repentance, when he realizes what he has done. For
example, a person might kill someone, because he thinks a
sharp-pointed spear has a button on it, and the action would
be involuntary and excusable (and he should be sorry for what
he has done). But the act would not be involuntary and excusable, if the agent did it as a result of ignorance that murder is morally wrong: he should know, and is culpable for not
knowing, that it is. Again, there is no distinction, in terms of
their voluntariness, between deliberate wrong acts and those
due to temper, as both considered judgements and irrational
feelings are part of human nature, and we must avoid wrong
actions, however they arise.

Aristotle notes that moral goodness is closely related to
choice, and he explores its nature. It follows deliberation,
which does not concern ends (which are what we wish for),
but the (best) practical means of realizing our ends: we say we
wish to be happy, but not that we choose to be. A statesman
does not deliberate about an end, such as whether to produce
law and order, but about the means of attaining it, and, provided it is attainable, sets about doing so. Having decided the
means, through deliberation, we direct our aim; and, as the
exercise of the moral virtues relates to means we have chosen,
as a result of deliberation, both virtue and vice are in our
power. We can do what is right and not do what is wrong, and
so we decide whether to be decent or worthless.

The view that our actions are in our power is (Aristotle
believes) borne out by the use of rewards and punishments,
which are designed to encourage right actions and restrain

wrong ones. People are responsible for their moral state, which reflects how they live. They develop qualities that correspond to their activities, making themselves unjust or licentious, for example, through dishonesty or drinking. However, while people who act unjustly or licentiously do so voluntarily, this does not mean they can stop, if they want to. Unjust and licentious persons had it in their power not to become so, in the first place, but may not be able to break free of the bad habits they have developed. But is it fair to hold people responsible for their moral defects in this way? Aristotle tackles what would now be described as the hard determinist view: that when people wrongly think that something is good, and aim at it, this is the result of their character, which is outside their control, while those who choose what is truly good have an inborn ability to do so. Aristotle dismisses such attempts to diminish human responsibility. Virtue and vice are both voluntary, because good and bad people have equal freedom in their actions, and perform all the means towards their ends voluntarily, even if they are not free in their choice of ends. Virtues are mean states and dispositions, which are voluntary, enable their possessor to perform the same sort of actions as those by which they were acquired; and to act as the right principle prescribes. However, actions and dispositions are not voluntary in the same sense, as we control the former throughout our lives, but the latter only at the beginning.

In the rest of Book III, Aristotle examines the virtues of courage and temperance in detail. While the rash man and the coward show excess or deficiency, the courageous man, having the right disposition, observes the mean, facing danger as a fine thing to do, and being undaunted as far as is humanly possible. He fears what human beings naturally fear (for example, there is nothing cowardly in a man dreading

brutality towards his wife and children), but faces it in the
right way, and for the sake of what is right and honourable,
as this is the end of virtue. He bears death and wounds, as
a fine thing to do, even though, as a virtuous person, death
is distressing him, because his life is so much worth living.
Aristotle also examines five dispositions that resemble courage: civic courage, which is grounded in moral virtue (the
citizens wish to do something noble); experience of risk (a
form of courage); spirit or mettle (regarded as courage, as it
involves being bold in the face of danger, but it should only
be so regarded if it includes deliberate choice); sanguineness,
which is not the same as courage (courageous people face up
to terrible things, but sanguine ones may run away if things
do not turn out as they expected); and ignorance (those acting
from ignorance only seem courageous).

Temperance is a virtue thought to belong to the irrational
part of the soul, and is a mean state in relation to physical
pleasures. With these, people err in enjoying the wrong objects, or enjoying things with abnormal intensity (people rarely desire pleasures less than they ought), while the licentious
display every form of excess. The temperate person does not
enjoy wrong pleasures, and is not distressed by the absence
of pleasures. He holds a mean position, moderately pursuing pleasures that are conducive to health, and which are not
dishonourable, or beyond his means, appreciating them as
the right principle directs. Aristotle regards licentiousness
as more voluntary than cowardice, because pain (which the
coward tries to avoid), unlike pleasure (which the licentious
person chooses), distracts the sufferer. Licentious people are
like spoilt children: just as children are impelled by their
desires, an irrational being has an insatiable appetite for what
gives pleasure, which indulging it intensifies, driving out

reason. Therefore, the reason must control the appetitive element, which needs to be in harmony with the former, so that
both have as their object attaining what is admirable.

Aristotle has already explained that human happiness is an
'activity of the soul', in accordance with 'a rational principle'
and the 'best and most perfect kind of virtue', and involves
pursuing and practising moral and intellectual virtues. Having discussed the moral virtues, he turns, in Book VI, to the
intellectual ones. Of course, the intellect (its calculative, as
opposed to its contemplative part) has a role in relation to the
moral virtues: good moral choices and conduct involve true
reasoning, as well as good character and right desire. There
is also the question of whether intellectual or moral virtue or
excellence is better.

Aristotle begins by examining the five states of mind, or
modes of thought, by which truth is reached. They are scientific knowledge (the process of induction or deduction
from known first principles); art (knowledge of how to make
things); prudence or practical wisdom (the ability to deliberate rightly about the things and actions that are good or bad
for human beings, and which will help them to lead a good
life); intuition (the ability to grasp the first principles on which
scientific knowledge is based); and (theoretical) wisdom (this
brings together intuition and scientific knowledge: the wise
man knows and understands both first principles and what
follows from them).

While Aristotle acknowledges that (theoretical) wisdom,
which concerns the 'most precious' kind of knowledge, is
superior to practical wisdom, the latter, which involves the
ability to deliberate, and knowledge of particular circumstances, plays a vital role in determining the means of achieving practical human goods. Indeed, he recognizes that those

who lack theoretical knowledge are often more effective in attaining these. Again, political science is a form of practical wisdom, so those who possess it will be equipped to look after the welfare of the wider community, as well as to secure their own good (although Aristotle notes that, whereas those who seek their own good are considered prudent, politicians are regarded as busybodies). Resourcefulness, which is correctness in estimating advantage with respect to the right object, the right means and the right time or opportunity, is also a kind of deliberation, while understanding, which is the ability to make (sound) judgements in matters requiring deliberation, belongs to the same sphere as practical wisdom.

Both (theoretical) wisdom and practical wisdom are intellectual virtues, which are desirable in themselves, and although the former does not deal with things that make human beings happy as such, given the knowledge with which it is concerned, it does produce happiness. As for the latter, Aristotle holds that the full performance of a human being's function depends on practical wisdom and moral virtue together: correct moral choices cannot be made without moral goodness, which identifies the end, or practical wisdom, which enables us to perform the actions that are the means to it. However, prudence is inferior to wisdom, and does not have authority over it: it does not give orders to it, but for its sake.

Finally (Book X), Aristotle turns to the life of happiness, starting with a discussion of pleasure. Some think pleasure is wholly bad, but Aristotle regards such views as exaggerated and designed to encourage people to attain the mean in relation to pleasures. It is undeniable that pleasure plays an important part in forming the character to like (or dislike) the right things, as people choose the pleasant and avoid pain, which leads some to regard it as the good. This was Eudoxus' opinion. He argued that the fact that all creatures are drawn to pleasure shows it is best for all, as each individual seeks its own good, and what is good for all, which all try to obtain, is the good. He also held that pleasure is desirable in itself, and that what is never chosen as a means to something else is the most desirable thing. However, Aristotle identifies a weakness in his further argument that adding pleasure to something good makes it more desirable, as any good thing is made more desirable by adding another good thing to it. This was how Plato (in the *Philebus*) disproved the view that pleasure is the good, by pointing out that intelligence makes the life of pleasure more desirable; and nothing can be the good, if adding something else to it makes it more desirable. Again, while it cannot be contended that what both rational and irrational creatures try to obtain is not a good, there are many things, such as memory and knowledge, which we wish to have, even if they bring no pleasure. Pleasure seems not to be the good, as not every pleasure is desirable, while some pleasures are superior in kind, or due to their sources.

What is Aristotle's conclusion? All our activities, both of thinking and sensing, have their corresponding pleasures, which are proper to them, and which intensify and perfect the activity. Thus, pleasure is essential to life: all creatures are drawn to it, directing their activities towards the objects, and through the faculties, they like best. So, it can be said that pleasure perfects these activities, and perfects life. However, this means that pleasure is not uniform, such that it can be regarded as the good for human beings. The pleasures proper to serious and bad activities are virtuous and vicious respectively, so pleasures differ in kind and quality, and we consider intellectual pleasures to be superior to sensuous ones. But the proper pleasure of every animal is exercising its proper function, and only investigation of human activities can show if there is one true pleasure that can be regarded as the proper pleasure of man.

So what is this? And what is the kind of life that will bring human beings most happiness or well-being? Aristotle sums up what he has said thus far. It is not a state, but an activity, and it must be chosen for its own sake, not for the sake of something else. But this applies to both 'actions that accord with goodness' and pleasant amusements. What about the latter? Aristotle is unequivocal that happiness must be distinguished from pleasant amusements. They may be pursued for their own sake, but they lead people to neglect their bodies and property, and although many people, regarded as happy, engage in them, they may not have experienced intellectual pleasures, so there is no reason for regarding their preference as a worthy choice. It is what good people think valuable (virtuous activity) that really is such; it would be absurd to live just for amusement. The happy life is lived according to goodness, suggesting seriousness, not amusement. Indeed, human activity is more serious in proportion as it is better, so serious activity is superior and more conducive to happiness.

Thus, perfect human happiness is found in the activity, which is proper to human beings, which accords with the highest virtue, and which is pleasantest for them. This is contemplative or intellectual activity, for the intellect is the highest thing in human beings, and apprehends the highest things they can know (such as philosophical and scientific truths). Further, while morally good people need others towards whom they can be just or benevolent, the wise man can practise contemplation alone, so it is a self-sufficient activity, which is appreciated for its own sake. Again, happiness is linked with leisure, but politics and war, in which the practical virtues are exercised, though noble and grand, leave no room for it, while, unlike intellectual activity, they aim at ends beyond themselves: politics, for example, is about securing the happiness of the politician and his fellow-citizens. As contemplation aims at no end beyond itself, and has a pleasure peculiar to it, it will be the source of perfect human happiness, as long as human beings have a full lifespan.

So, the happiest human beings are those who lead the contemplative life, and the more they engage in intellectual activity, the happier they will be. What about moral activity? Does this also bring happiness? Aristotle accepts that it does, but a life spent practising the moral virtues produces a lower level of happiness. Moral goodness is intimately connected with the human feelings, so living in conformity with them, and its associated happiness, fits in with our physical nature and also with the fact that we lead our lives as members of society. However, unlike the intellectual life, the life of moral goodness requires resources: for example, the liberal man needs money to be liberal. Another argument for happiness being contemplative activity is that, of all human activities, it is the one most akin to that of the gods, and, of all living creatures, only human beings have this activity in common with them. However, being human, people also require health and food, but (Aristotle maintains) happiness does not depend on external goods: neither intellectual activity, nor moral conduct, requires extensive material possessions. Indeed, happy people tend to have a moderate quantity of external goods, to live temperate lives, and to do the finest deeds.

Aristotle has set out his ethical theory, but how is it to be put into practice? He accepts that the most important thing may not be outlining happiness and the intellectual and moral virtues, but becoming good. However, given the intellectual and moral limitations of the majority, developing a (modest) degree of goodness in people may be all that is achievable. He feels that education in goodness is best undertaken by the state, which needs to regulate the upbringing and activities of its citizens, and, as people respond better to compulsion and punishment than argument, to punish the disobedient, as well as appealing to the finer feelings of those who have already developed good habits. However, as most states neglect these responsibilities, parents may need to instruct their children in goodness; and such instruction has the advantages of being influenced by natural affection, and, as there is individual attention, being more accurate. But if the state does (as it should) involve itself in making people good, by enabling them to acquire intellectual and moral virtues, students and teachers of ethics will need to acquire knowledge of legislation and political science. They should study laws and constitutions closely, as this will enable them to discover why some states are better governed than others; to determine the best kind of constitution and system of laws; and to make their philosophy of human conduct as complete as possible.

The Nicomachean Ethics has had an enormous influence on thinking about ethics, and on the course of moral philosophy, for almost two and a half thousand years. It is hard to fault Aristotle's approach: the best way to discover the supreme good for human beings, and what constitutes their happiness, does seem to be by looking at their nature and function, in order to determine what sort of beings they are; and, as human beings are rational beings, and also social beings, who interact with others in society, the intellectual and moral virtues clearly do have an important part to play in ensuring human well-being and happiness. His concept of the moral virtues as being like crafts, which people can acquire through developing the habit of right conduct from an early age, so that they will be able to lead morally good lives, is an attractive and persuasive one. Unfortunately, as he points out (and this has been true across the centuries), both the state and parents tend to neglect their responsibilities for the moral education of children.

But Aristotle's view that the happiest human beings are those who lead the contemplative life (and that the more people engage in intellectual activity, the happier they will be), while a life devoted to practising the moral virtues produces a lower level of happiness, seems to reflect the priorities of a life that was spent in pursuit of philosophical truth and scientific research. It is highly debatable, as it can be argued that the greatest human happiness is found in the practice of moral goodness: in helping others, particularly those who are suffering. Thus, many people would consider the moral virtues to be more important than the intellectual ones, because they determine the way we relate to, and treat, others, while some would maintain that ethics' sole concern is with our conduct towards other people.

Indeed, the precedence Aristotle gives to individual intellectual activity may appear selfish. He is concerned with the happiness the individual can attain, through engaging in intellectual activity by himself, and thinks that the wise man, practising the intellectual virtues, has an advantage over morally good people, practising the moral virtues: his activity is self-sufficient, while morally good people need others towards whom they can be just or benevolent (and the necessary material resources). What is lacking here is altruistic concern with the happiness of others: there is no mention of the utilitarian idea of actively promoting general happiness. On the other hand, cultivation of the intellectual virtues enables people to exercise the moral virtues and practise moral goodness more effectively: while correct moral choices cannot be made without moral goodness, which identifies the end, it is practical wisdom, an intellectual virtue, which enables us to perform the actions that are the means of achieving it.

Some Issues to Consider

- Aristotle believes everything has an end or purpose, which is determined by its nature or function; the (supreme) good for all things, including human beings, is to fulfil this end or purpose.
- The task of ethics is to identify what is the supreme or highest good for human beings, and this has an important bearing on how people lead their lives, as they are more likely to achieve their aim if they have a definite target.
- Aristotle holds that the supreme end or purpose, and therefore, the supreme good, for human beings, is happiness, because it is a final end, which is pursued for its own sake, not for the sake of anything else, is completely satisfying, and makes life desirable.
- Aristotle identifies three main types of life that are held to be happy: the pleasure-seeking or hedonistic; one devoted to pursuit of political honours; and the contemplative life.
- Do you agree with Aristotle's criticisms of the pleasure-seeking life and a life devoted to pursuit of political honours?
- Aristotle maintains that we discover what constitutes happiness for human beings by looking at their nature and function, and that what distinguishes them from plants and animals is that they are rational beings.
- For Aristotle, human happiness is an activity of the soul,

in accordance with a rational principle and the best and most perfect kind of virtue.

- The appetitive/desiring and rational proper parts of the soul have their corresponding classes of virtues or excellences, the moral (those of character) and the intellectual; human happiness consists in pursuing and practising these.

- Aristotle explicitly rejects Plato's theory of the forms and the form of the good as the source of reality, truth and goodness.

- Do you agree with Aristotle that both ethics and politics are not exact sciences, and that we should not look for more precision in them than their nature permits?

- Aristotle thinks a good man's function is to lead his life well, and he will be happy throughout it, as he will spend it in virtuous conduct and contemplation; but it is only when his life is complete, and it is clear that this is how he has spent his life, that he can rightly be called happy.

- Moral virtues, like crafts, are acquired by habit: in the same way that people become good builders by building well, they become just by performing just acts, so the habits people develop from the earliest age, through the actions they perform, play a vital part in determining their moral dispositions.

- Aristotle maintains that right conduct is incompatible with excess or deficiency in feelings or actions, which destroy our moral qualities.

- He thinks our attitude to pleasures and pains indicates our degree of moral goodness: pleasures make us behave badly, and pains deter us from fine actions, and we can become bad through them, by seeking, or shunning, the wrong ones, so we need to develop the right attitude towards them.

Some Issues to Consider

- Do you agree with Aristotle that a virtuous act is not virtuous, merely because it has a certain external quality, but only if the agent knows what he is doing; chooses to perform the action for its own sake; and does so from a permanent disposition to act in that way?

- According to Aristotle, a virtue is a condition of being well- or ill-disposed towards something, and being inclined to act towards it in a particular way; moral virtues are dispositions that make someone a good man and enable him to perform his function well.

- The doctrine of the mean refers to a relative mean between excess and deficiency that the moral virtues, which concern feelings and actions, aim to hit.

- Aristotle explains that the mean does not apply to feelings and actions like malice and murder, which are evil in themselves, while it is not always equidistant between the extremes of excess and deficiency.

- Aristotle suggests rules we can follow to help us hit the mean.

- Involuntary actions arise from external compulsion or ignorance, but Aristotle accepts that the dividing-line between voluntary and involuntary actions is not absolutely clear-cut: there are mixed actions, where the agent has the power to perform, or not perform, the action, but is forced into a wrong action, which, in normal circumstances, he would not choose to do.

- Aristotle does not think that such situations excuse any action the agent performs, however bad: people would, and should, rather die than do some things, and they are blamed or praised according to the extent to which they have, or have not, yielded to compulsion.

- Is it only ignorance of particular circumstances, as when

the agent is mistaken about what he is doing, not ignorance of a moral principle, that makes an act involuntary?

- Aristotle notes that moral goodness is closely related to choice: this is the result of deliberation, which does not concern ends, which are what we wish for, but the (best) practical means of realizing our ends.
- Aristotle holds that people are responsible for their moral state, which reflects how they live, but while people who act wrongly do so voluntarily, this does not mean they can stop, if they want to, as they may not be able to break free of the bad habits they have developed.
- The courageous person fears what human beings naturally fear, but faces it in the right way, and for the sake of what is right and honourable.
- The temperate person moderately pursues pleasures that are conducive to health, and which are not dishonourable, or beyond his means.
- According to Aristotle, there are five states of mind, or modes of thought, by which truth is reached: scientific knowledge; art; prudence or practical wisdom; intuition; and (theoretical) wisdom.
- Aristotle holds that (theoretical) wisdom, which concerns the most precious kind of knowledge, is superior to practical wisdom or prudence.
- Aristotle thinks that the full performance of a human being's function depends on practical wisdom and moral virtue together: correct moral choices cannot be made without moral goodness, which identifies the end, or practical wisdom, which enables us to perform the actions that are the means to it.
- Eudoxus argued that the fact that all creatures are drawn to pleasure shows it is best for all, as each individual seeks its

own good; and what is good for all, which all try to obtain, is the good.

- Aristotle points out that Plato disproved the view that pleasure is the good, by pointing out that intelligence makes the life of pleasure more desirable, and nothing can be the good, if adding something else to it makes it more desirable.

- Aristotle observes that all our activities, both of thinking and sensing, have their corresponding pleasures, which are proper to them, and which intensify and perfect the activity.

- However, this means that pleasure is not uniform, such that it can be regarded as the good for human beings, as pleasures differ in kind and quality.

- Aristotle is unequivocal that happiness must be distinguished from pleasant amusements: they may be pursued for their own sake, but they lead people to neglect their bodies and property, and, although many people, regarded as happy, engage in them, they may not have experienced intellectual pleasures, so there is no reason for regarding their preference as a worthy choice.

- Aristotle contends that perfect human happiness is found in contemplative or intellectual activity, which is the activity proper to human beings, for the intellect is the highest thing in human beings, and apprehends the highest things they can know (such as philosophical and scientific truths).

- Do you agree that a life spent practising the moral virtues produces a lower level of happiness than the contemplative life?

- Aristotle believes that, of all human activities, contemplative activity is the one most akin to that of the gods.

- Do you agree with Aristotle that neither intellectual

activity, nor moral conduct, depends on extensive material possessions?

- Aristotle accepts that the most important thing may not be outlining happiness and the intellectual and moral virtues, but becoming good.
- Aristotle feels that education in goodness is best undertaken by the state, which needs to regulate the upbringing and activities of its citizens, but as most states neglect these responsibilities, parents may need to instruct their children in goodness.
- Aristotle argues that students and teachers of ethics need to study laws and constitutions closely.

Suggestions for Further Reading

Aristotle, *The Eudemian Ethics* (Books 1, 2 and 8), trans. M. Wood, second edition, Oxford: Oxford University Press, 1992.

Aristotle, *Metaphysics*, trans. H. Lansson-Tancred, new edition, London: Penguin Books, 1998.

Aristotle, *The Nicomachean Ethics*, trans. J. A. K. Thomson (notes and appendices by H. Tredennick, Introduction and Further Reading by J. Barnes), revised edition, London: Penguin Books, 1976.

Aristotle, *The Nicomachean Ethics*, trans. D. Ross (revised by J. L. Ackrill and J. O. Urmson), Oxford: Oxford University Press, 1998.

Aristotle, *Politics*, trans. T. A. Sinclair and T. J. Saunders, revised edition, London: Penguin Books, 1998.

J. L. Ackrill, *Aristotle the Philosopher*, Oxford: Oxford University Press, 1981.

J. Barnes, *Aristotle*, second edition, Oxford: Oxford University Press, 2000.

S. Broadie and C. J. Rowe, *Aristotle: Nicomachean Ethics*, Oxford: Oxford University Press, 2002.

K. J. Dover, *Greek Popular Morality in the Time of Plato and Aristotle*, Indianapolis: Hackett Publishing Company, 1980.

M. I. Finley, *The Ancient Greeks*, London: Penguin Books, 1991.

W. F. R. Hardie, *Aristotle's Ethical Theory*, second edition, Oxford: Oxford University Press, 1980.

T. H. Irwin, *Aristotle: Nicomachean Ethics*, second edition, Indianapolis: Hackett Publishing Company, 1999.

J. S. Mill, *Utilitarianism*, ed. G. Sher, Indianapolis/Cambridge: Hackett Publishing Company, 2001.

Plato, *Philebus*, trans. D. Frede, Indianapolis: Hackett Publishing Company, 1993.

Plato, *The Republic*, trans. H. D. P. Lee, second edition (revised and reissued with new Further Reading), London: Penguin Books, 2003.

J. O. Urmson, *Aristotle's Ethics*, Oxford: Oxford University Press, 1987.

Detailed Summary of Aristotle's
The Nicomachean Ethics

Book I

The Object of Life (pp. 3–30)

*i Every rational activity aims at some end or good. One end
(like one activity) may be subordinate to another (pp. 3–4)*

Every 'art' and 'action' is thought to 'aim at some good'; thus,
'**the good**' is that 'at which all things aim' (p. 3). But '**ends**'
differ: some are 'activities', others 'results distinct from the
activities' (p. 3). Where ends exist, 'distinct from the actions',
the 'results' are 'superior to the activities' (p. 3). As there are
'many actions, arts and sciences', there are many ends: for
example, that of 'medical science' is health (p. 3). However,
many arts come under a '**single faculty**', as 'making bridles'
comes under 'horsemanship', which comes under '**military
science**' (p. 3). In these cases, the ends of the latter must be
'preferred', as it is for their sake that the former 'are pursued'
(p. 3). If 'our activities' have an end that 'we **want for its own
sake**', this must be 'the good, that is, the supreme good', and
it will help us greatly in the 'conduct of our lives': we are 'more
likely to achieve our aim' with 'a target' (p. 4).

ii The science that studies the supreme good for man is politics (pp. 4–5)

It seems that the 'most authoritative' science is '**politics**', which determines the 'subjects' to be 'taught in states' (p. 4). Everything else, such as 'war' and 'property management', comes under it (p. 4). As it 'lays down what we should do' and 'refrain' from, and uses 'the other sciences', 'this end must be the good for man' (p. 4). For, even if the good 'of the individual' and 'the community' coincide, that of the latter seems 'finer and more sublime' (pp. 4–5). This is 'the aim of our investigation': it is 'a kind of **political science**' (p. 5).

iii Politics is not an exact science (pp. 5–6)

'Our account of this science' will be 'adequate', if it attains the 'clarity' that the 'subject-matter allows' (p. 5). The 'instances of morally fine and just conduct', with which political science is concerned, show great 'difference and variety', and so may be thought to be so by '**convention**', not '**nature**' (p. 5). Goods also involve 'variety': they can be hurtful, as people are destroyed 'by their courage' (p. 5). Thus, we must be 'satisfied' with a 'broad outline of the truth' (p. 5). The 'trained mind' does not look for 'more precision' in a subject than 'the nature of that subject permits', and it would be as 'reasonable' to expect '**logical demonstrations**' from a **rhetorician** as 'mere plausibility from a mathematician' (p. 5).

The student should have some general knowledge and experience of life (p. 6). Everyone 'judges rightly what he understands', so 'the man with a general education' is a 'good critic in general' (p. 6). A 'young man' is not 'fit' to study 'political science', as 'he is not versed in the practical business of life' (p. 6). He also 'tends to follow his feelings', and will not benefit from it, 'since the object' is 'not knowledge but action' (p. 6). But for those who 'act in accordance with principle', knowing about these subjects 'will be of great advantage' (p. 6).

iv The end is no doubt happiness, but views of happiness differ (pp. 6–8)

Both 'ordinary and cultured people' agree that the 'highest of all practical goods' is 'happiness', which they identify 'with living well' (pp. 6–7). But they differ as to what it is, with the former group thinking it is something 'obvious', such as 'pleasure or money' (p. 5). And, even 'the same person' may change 'his opinion', saying it is 'health' when he is ill, and 'money' when he is 'hard up' (p. 7). Some 'have held' that, 'above these particular goods', there is **another which is good in itself and the cause of whatever goodness there is in all these others**' (p. 7). What are the 'most prevalent' views (p. 7)?

Learners must start from beliefs that are accepted or at least familiar (pp. 7–8). **Plato** was right to point out the 'difference' between arguments '*from* or *to* **first principles**' (p. 7). Things are 'known in two senses': 'to us' and 'absolutely'; and we must begin with the former (p. 7). One, who is to study 'ethics' or 'political science' seriously, needs to have been 'well trained in his habits', for the 'starting-point is the *fact*', and if this is 'sufficiently clear', it will not be necessary to find 'the reason why' (pp. 7–8).

v The three types of life. Neither pleasure nor public honour seems to be an adequate end; the contemplative life will be considered later (pp. 8–9)

The 'masses and the most vulgar' people believe 'the good or happiness is pleasure' (p. 8). There are three main 'types of life': the 'one just mentioned', the 'political' and the '**con-templative**' (p. 8). The 'masses' prefer to live 'a bovine existence', as do many in 'positions of power' (p. 8). 'Cultured people' identify 'the good with **honour**', which is 'the goal of political life' (p. 8). However, this seems too 'superficial' an answer, as honour depends on the giver, rather than the one 'who receives it', whereas we feel that 'the good is something proper to its possessor' (p. 9). Also, men seek 'to be honoured' for their goodness (p. 9). They regard it as 'superior to honour', so perhaps, this is 'the end pursued in public life' (p. 9). However, possessing goodness seems 'compatible even with being asleep', or leading a 'life of inactivity' (p. 9). The 'contemplative life' will be considered below (p. 7).

Wealth is not the good we are after, because it 'serves only as a means' to 'something else' (p. 9). The 'earlier suggestions' are 'more likely ends', as they are 'appreciated on their own account', but even they are 'inadequate', and can be 'dismissed' (p. 9).

vi There cannot be a universal good such as Plato held to be the culmination of his theory of forms (pp. 10–13)

We should examine 'the **universal**', although 'such a course' is made more 'awkward', because of 'the **forms**' (p. 10). Those who 'introduced this theory' did not 'posit ideas of classes in which they recognized degrees of priority' (p. 10). But things are called 'good' in the categories of '**substance**', '**quality**' and '**relation**'; and, as that which 'exists in its own right, namely substance, is by nature prior' to the relative, there cannot be any 'common idea in these cases' (p. 10). Also, as things are called 'good in as many senses as they are said to exist', as 'in the category of substance (e.g. god or mind)', in 'quality (the virtues)', in 'quantity (what is moderate)', in 'relation (what is useful)', and so on, there cannot be 'a single universal common to all cases' (p. 10). It would also mean there would be 'one science of all good things', but there are 'more than one', even in things that 'fall under one category' (pp. 10–11). And what is meant 'by speaking of a thing-itself' (p. 11)? If the 'definition of man' is 'the same' in 'man and in man-himself', what is 'good and the **good-itself**' will not 'differ *qua* good', while 'good' will not be 'any more good by being **eternal**' (p. 11).

Further, 'only those g**oods that are pursued or esteemed in their own right**', are 'called good in virtue of one form': those that are just a **means to good** are called 'good' in a 'different sense' (p. 11). We shall 'separate' the things 'good in themselves' from the '**merely useful**', to determine whether they are 'called good in virtue of one idea' (pp. 11–12). Many things can be regarded as '**good in themselves**', such as 'sight', 'pleasures' and 'honours' (12). But are they? Or is nothing good in itself, 'except the idea' (p. 12)? If so, the 'class will be purposeless' (p. 12). Further, if they are 'good in themselves', the 'definition of good' would have to be 'the same in them all' (p. 12). But, as they all have different definitions 'in respect of goodness', 'good is not a common characteristic corresponding to one idea' (p. 12).

So, do 'all goods derive from or contribute to one good', or are they 'good by analogy' (p. 12)? This 'subject' should be considered elsewhere (p. 12). Even if 'the goodness that is predicated in common' is 'one thing' that exists separately, it cannot be 'acquired by man' (p. 12). Perhaps, we should achieve knowledge of 'goods that *can* be acquired', so as to know the things that are 'good *for us*' (p. 12). However, this clashes with the way the 'practical sciences' work, as these aim at a good, but not 'knowledge of it' (pp. 12–13). For example, how would

a 'weaver or a joiner' benefit from knowing 'this good-itself'
(p. 13)? Again, 'a doctor' does not study 'health in this way': he
is concerned with 'the health of a human being' (p. 13).

*vii What is the good for man? It must be the ultimate end
or object of human life: something that is in itself completely
satisfying. Happiness fits this description (pp. 13–17)*

The 'good' we are looking for seems to 'vary with the action
or art' (p. 13). The 'good of each particular one' is the *'end'*,
for which 'everything else is done': in 'medicine', it is 'health',
'in strategy, victory', and so on (p. 13). Thus, if one thing is
'the end of all actions', it is 'the **practical good**' (p. 13). However, we must be precise: some of the ends 'we choose', such
as 'wealth', are 'means to something else', and, unlike 'the
supreme good', not '**final ends**' (pp. 13–14). An end, which
is 'never choosable', because of another, is 'more final' than
those 'choosable because of it as well as for their own sakes'
(p. 14). That end, which is only 'choosable for its own sake', is
'final without any qualification' (p. 14).

Now, '**happiness**', which is chosen 'for itself', is regarded as
'just such an end' (p. 14). We choose 'honour' or 'intelligence',
for example, 'partly for themselves', but also 'for the sake of
our happiness' (p. 14). Happiness, however, is never chosen
for *'their* sake' or for 'any other reason' (p. 14). Again, it is 'generally accepted' that the 'perfect good is self-sufficient': that
is, one that 'by itself makes life desirable'; and 'happiness is
such a thing' (p. 14). It is not made 'more desirable' by adding
another good to it, to make a greater '**sum of goods**'; it is 'the
end to which our actions are directed' (pp. 14–15).

*But what is happiness? If we consider what the function of
man is, we find that happiness is a virtuous activity of the soul*

(pp. 15–16). How do we define happiness? Perhaps, we can do so by 'grasping what is the function of man' (p. 15). The 'goodness' of any 'class of men', who perform a specific 'activity', such as sculptors, lies in 'performance of that function' (p. 15). Is man 'as such' a 'functionless being' (p. 15)? But, in the same way that 'our members', like the 'eye and hand', have 'some function', should we not take it that a human being has a function 'over and above' any particular ones (p. 15)? We are seeking man's *'proper* function', so must exclude 'nutrition and growth', and **'sentient life'**, which he shares with plants and animals (p. 15). Thus, the 'function of man' must be 'an activity of the **soul**', in accordance with 'a **rational principle**' (p. 16). Now, if we take it that the function of an 'individual', and a 'good individual of the same kind', is 'generically the same' (a harpist's function is to 'play the harp', that of a good one to 'play it well'), and assume that man's function is as stated above, a good man's function is to lead this 'kind of life' 'well and rightly' (p. 16). In 'conclusion', the 'good for man is an activity of the soul in accordance with virtue', or the 'best and most perfect kind' of virtue, which must take place 'in a complete lifetime' (p. 16).

This sketch can be elaborated later, but great precision is not to be expected (pp. 16–17). This is an 'outline account of the good'; we can 'fill in the details' later (p. 16). We must also remember what we said before, and seek only the 'degree of exactness' the 'subject-matter' permits, and which is 'appropriate to the investigation': we must not allow 'the swamping of main by side issues' (p. 17). We do not require 'the explanation' of everything: in some cases, as with 'first principles', exhibiting 'the *fact*' will suffice, as it is 'a starting-point' (p. 17). It is generally agreed that 'the beginning is more than half the whole task' (p. 17).

viii Our view of happiness is supported by popular beliefs
(pp. 18–20)

We must examine our principle not only as 'reached logically', but 'in the light of what is commonly said about it'
(p. 18). Our 'definition' is supported by the fact that 'goods'
have been put into three classes: '(1) external, (2) of the soul
and (3) of the body' (p. 18). We say that those 'of the soul' are
good in the 'fullest sense' (p. 18). We are also right to say that
'the end consists in certain actions', as this 'puts it among
the goods of the soul' (p. 18). Our definition is also supported
by the belief that the 'happy man lives and fares well', as we
have described 'a kind of good life'; and it includes 'all the
required constituents of happiness', which some think is
'virtue', others 'prudence', and so on (p. 18). These views are a
mix of long-held 'popular beliefs' and those of 'distinguished
men' (p. 18).

An important point is whether we think 'the supreme good'
is *'possession'* of virtue, or its *'exercise'*, for the former, a *'state'*,
could be 'present' in someone, but effect no 'good result', which
would not be so if it is an *'activity'* (pp. 18–19). And such a life
is 'in itself pleasant', for 'each individual finds pleasure in that
of which he is said to be fond' (p. 19). 'Virtuous actions' are
pleasant 'in themselves', and give pleasure to 'the lover of virtue', so he does not require pleasure to be added to his life 'as
a sort of accessory' (p. 19). One who does not 'delight in fine
actions' (as the just man does in 'acting justly') is not even
'good', for, if the good man's judgement 'is right', as we have
said, they are 'pleasurable in themselves' and 'good and fine'
in the 'highest degree' (p. 19). Thus, 'happiness is the best,
the finest, the most pleasurable thing of all' (p. 19). However,
it needs 'external goods', as it is hard to perform 'fine deeds'
without 'any resources', while people are not happy if, for ex-

ample, they are 'ugly' or 'solitary', suggesting that it requires 'this sort of prosperity' (p. 20).

ix How is happiness acquired? (pp. 20–2)

Is happiness 'learnt', 'acquired by habituation', or is it a 'divine dispensation' (p. 20)? It would be a suitable 'gift of the **gods**', and, if it is, in fact, 'acquired by moral goodness', and through 'training', it is certainly 'one of our most divine possessions' (pp. 20–1). That it is acquired in this way would mean it will be 'widely shared', as it is attainable by anyone, who is not 'handicapped by some incapacity for goodness' (p. 21). It is 'better' that it should be won, in this way, than come 'by chance' (p. 21). This view fits in with our 'definition' of happiness as 'a kind of virtuous activity of soul', whereas 'other goods' 'contribute to it', or 'serve as its instruments' (p. 21). We also said that political science's end is 'the highest good', the main 'concern' of which is to 'endue the **citizens**' with such 'qualities' as 'virtue and the readiness to do fine deeds' (p. 21). We do not talk of animals or children as happy, for the former are incapable of 'this sort of activity', while 'age debars' the latter from it: happiness requires 'a complete life', as well as 'complete goodness' (p. 21). But people who have prospered in life, like **Priam**, may suffer 'great misfortunes': we would not call them 'happy' (pp. 21–2).

x Is it only when his life is completed that a man can rightly be called happy? (pp. 22–5)

Is no one happy while 'alive', meaning that, as **Solon** put it, we must 'look to the end'? However, it seems an 'utter paradox' to say a man is 'really happy' when dead, given that we have defined happiness as 'a kind of activity' (p. 22). But it is difficult to deny that the dead are happy, as it is 'popularly believed that some good and evil' touches them: it seems 'absurd' to maintain that they are unaffected by the 'experiences of the descendants' (p. 22). On the other hand, if we 'call a man happy, not because he *is* but because he *was*', it would be equally absurd to contend that 'the fact cannot be truly stated of him' when he is (p. 23). 'Changes of fortune' are beside the point, because 'success and failure in life' do not depend on them, as they are 'merely complements': it is 'virtuous activities' that determine our happiness (p. 23). The 'happy man' will be 'happy throughout his life', as he will spend most of it 'in virtuous conduct and contemplation' (p. 23).

The 'nobility' of a man who bears 'heavy disasters' patiently, due to his 'high and generous nature', 'shines through' (p. 24). A 'truly happy' man cannot 'become miserable', for he will never do 'hateful and mean' things, nor will he be 'variable and inconstant', as 'ordinary misfortunes' will not dislodge him 'from his happiness' (p. 24). So, the 'happy man' is 'active in accordance with complete virtue', and has an adequate supply of 'external goods' through 'a complete life' and when he dies: for happiness is 'an *end* in every way utterly final and complete' (pp. 24–5). Thus, the living who have, and will continue to have, these 'qualifications' are 'supremely happy – but with a human happiness' (p. 25).

xi Are the dead affected by the fortunes of those who survive them? (pp. 25–6)

The idea that 'the dead' are unaffected by their descendants' 'fortunes' is 'contrary to **accepted beliefs**' (p. 25). But 'experiences are so many' and varied that a 'broad outline' of this matter will suffice (p. 25). A person's 'misfortunes', and those of his friends, sometimes exert a 'powerful influence upon his life', but, at others, a 'trivial' one (p. 25). So, it is debatable whether or not 'the departed' participate in 'good or its opposite' (p. 25). We can probably infer from the foregoing that, while the dead are 'affected to some extent' by the fortunes of those 'they love', the 'effect of good or evil' reaching them will be 'faint and slight': certainly, it will not be enough to make the 'unhappy happy', or vice versa (pp. 25–6).

xii Is happiness to be praised as a means or valued as an end?
(pp. 26–7)

Is happiness to be '*praised*' or '*valued*' (p. 26)? Well, we praise things for having a 'certain relation to something else' (p. 26). We praise 'the good man and virtue', due to 'the actions and effects that they produce': and the same is true (although it is 'absurd' to refer them to 'our standards) of 'praise addressed to the gods' (p. 26). But, if praise 'belongs to what is relative', the 'best things' demand 'something greater and better', as when we call the gods 'blessed' (p. 26). **Eudoxus** argued that pleasure's not 'being praised' is evidence of its superiority to other 'goods', as are 'gods and the good' (p. 27). '**Encomia**' are 'directed towards achievements' (p. 27). Happiness is a 'first principle': we do everything 'for its sake', and hold that 'the first principle and cause of what is good is precious and divine' (p. 27).

xiii To understand what moral goodness is we must study the soul of man (pp. 27–30)

We will be able to 'form a view about happiness' by examining the 'nature of virtue' (p. 27). After all, the 'true statesman' studies 'this subject' thoroughly, as he wants his 'fellow-citizens' to be 'good and law-abiding' (p. 27). Our concern is with 'human goodness', that is 'goodness' of 'the soul', for we are interested in 'the good' or 'happiness *for man*' (p. 28). Thus, the statesman needs to 'study the soul', but 'with a view to politics' and only to a 'sufficient' degree for that purpose (p. 28).

The several faculties of the soul distinguished (pp. 28–30). We can utilize 'the results' of **psychology**: we know that the **soul is 'part rational and part irrational'** (p. 28). One part of the latter, 'the **vegetative**', is common to 'everything that receives nourishment', and so 'has no part in human goodness' (pp. 28–9). However, there is another 'irrational' element in the soul, which 'strains against the rational', as when the 'impulses of the **incontinent** take them in the contrary direction' (p. 29). But it 'seems to be receptive of reason', as, in 'the continent man', it obeys reason, and is completely in 'harmony' with it in 'brave' and 'temperate' men (pp. 29–30). So, there are 'two parts' of the 'irrational part of the soul', with the '**desiderative**' or '**appetitive**' **part** participating 'in reason', in that it obeys it, as is shown by our use of 'reproof and encouragement' (p. 30). On the other hand, if we class the 'appetitive part' as 'rational', we have two rational parts, with the relation of the appetitive to the rational part 'proper' being that of 'a child' paying 'attention to its father' (p. 30).

There are two corresponding 'classes' of virtue: 'intellectual', such as 'wisdom', 'understanding and prudence', which we refer to when we praise someone for 'his state of mind'; and 'moral', such as 'liberality and temperance', which relate to 'a man's *character*' (p. 30).

Book II

Moral Goodness (pp. 31–49)

i Moral virtues, like crafts, are acquired by practice and habituation (pp. 31–2)

Virtue is either 'intellectual' or 'moral' (p. 31). The first originates in, and develops from, 'instruction' (p. 31). The second results from 'habit', which is why we call it *'ethos'* (p. 31). Thus, the **'moral virtues'** are not 'engendered in us by nature', which cannot be made to 'behave differently by habituation': we cannot 'train fire to burn downwards' (p. 31). They are engendered 'neither *by* nor *contrary to* nature': we are 'constituted by nature to receive them', but their 'full development' is 'due to habit' (p. 31). Indeed, with all the **'faculties'** nature gives us, we first acquire 'the potentialities', and then actualize them (p. 31). As with 'the arts', we acquire the virtues 'by first exercising them': people become 'builders by building', and 'become just by performing just acts' (p. 32). The intention of 'every legislator' is to make his 'citizens good by habituation' (p. 32).

Further, the 'means' of bringing about 'any form of excellence' are the 'same as those that destroy it' (p. 32). People become 'good builders' by 'building well', and 'bad ones' by doing so 'badly' (p. 32). If this were not the case, they would not require teachers, but would be *'born either* good or bad' (p. 32). It is the same with the virtues: it is, for example, 'our dealings' with others that makes us 'just or unjust', while we become **'temperate** and patient' by so conducting ourselves (p. 32). Thus, we must give our activities 'a certain quality', because it is 'their characteristics' that 'determine the resulting **dispositions**' (p. 32). The 'sort of habits we form from the earliest age' matter a great deal (p. 32).

ii In practical science so much depends upon particular circumstances that only general rules can be given (pp. 33–5)

As the 'branch of philosophy' we are studying concerns 'how to become good men', not knowledge of 'what goodness is', we must consider how we should perform 'our actions', as these 'determine our dispositions' (p. 33). Now, we may assume that we should 'act according to the **right principle**', but, as stated before, 'any account of conduct' must only 'be stated in outline', as befits the 'subject-matter' (p. 33). Questions of conduct have 'as little fixity' as those about 'what is healthful', and if this is so with 'the general rule', it is even truer of its 'application to particular problems' (p. 33). As in medicine, we have to think for ourselves what 'the circumstances demand' (p. 33).

A cardinal rule: right conduct is incompatible with excess or deficiency in feelings and actions (p. 34). Moral qualities are 'destroyed by deficiency and excess' (p. 34). Just as, for example, 'eating and drinking too much or too little destroy health', the same applies to 'courage and the other virtues' (p. 34). One who 'fears everything and stands up to nothing' turns into 'a coward', while one 'afraid of nothing at all', who 'marches up to every danger', 'becomes foolhardy': 'temperance and courage are destroyed by excess and deficiency and preserved by **the mean**' (p. 34).

Our virtues are exercised in the same kinds of action as gave rise to them (pp. 34–5). Just as the 'same sort of actions' both promote and destroy the virtues, the 'activities that flow from them' also 'consist in the same sort of actions' (p. 34). Thus, we 'become temperate', by 'refraining from pleasures', and are 'most able to abstain from pleasures', when we have 'become temperate' (pp. 34–5).

*iii The pleasure or pain that actions cause the agent may serve
as an index of moral progress, since good conduct consists in a
proper attitude towards pleasure and pain (pp. 35–7)*

The pleasure or pain accompanying 'people's acts' indicates
'their dispositions': for example, one who 'faces danger gladly' is brave, whereas one who 'feels distressed is a coward'
(p. 35). 'Moral goodness' is to do with 'pleasures and pains',
as the first makes us 'behave badly', while the second leads
us to 'shrink from fine actions'; this is why Plato pointed out
'the importance' of being 'trained' in feeling 'joy and grief at
the right things' (p. 35). Punishment utilizes 'pleasures and
pains', and people 'become bad' through them, by 'seeking (or
shunning) the wrong ones' (pp. 35–6).

'There are three factors that make for choice' (the 'fine',
'advantageous' and 'pleasant'), and three for 'avoidance'
('the base', 'harmful' and 'painful'): the good man goes right
with these, while the bad one goes wrong (p. 36). 'Pleasure
and pain' are also 'the standards' by which 'we regulate our
actions', and they greatly affect our 'conduct' (p. 36). **Heraclitus** says it is hard to 'fight against pleasure', so 'the whole
concern of both morality and political science must be with
pleasures and pains': one treating them 'rightly will be good',
while one treating them 'wrongly will be bad' (pp. 36–7). This
is a 'sufficient statement that virtue is concerned with pains
and pleasures' (p. 37).

*iv Acts that are incidentally virtuous distinguished from
those that are done knowingly, of choice and from a virtuous
disposition (pp. 37–8)*

But how can we say that people 'must perform just actions' to
become just (p. 37)? If 'they do what is just', they are so already,

in the same way that, if they use words 'correctly they are already literate' (p. 37). But the 'analogy' with 'the arts' does not hold: 'virtuous acts are not done' in a 'just or temperate way merely because *they* have a certain quality, but only if the agent also acts in a certain state': that is (1) 'knows what he is doing'; (2) 'chooses it for its own sake'; and (3) does so from a 'permanent disposition' (p. 37). What makes someone 'just or temperate' is not merely his doing such acts, but doing them as 'just and temperate men do' (p. 38). Thus, it is 'right to say' that people become just by performing just acts; and there is no possibility 'of any man's becoming good by not doing them' (p. 38). But this is not what 'most people' do: they rely on theory, and think 'they are being philosophical' (p. 38).

v   In order to define virtue we must decide to what class or genus it belongs. It is not a feeling or a faculty, but a disposition (pp. 38–9)

What is virtue? It must be one of the 'three kinds of modification', 'found in the soul': **feelings, faculties and dispositions** (p. 38). By the first, I mean 'desire, anger, fear', and so on; by the second, our being able to have 'the feelings in question'; by the third, the 'conditions' of being 'well or ill disposed' towards them: our disposition 'towards anger' is 'bad' if 'our tendency is too strong or too weak', but 'good' if 'moderate' (pp. 38–9). Neither our virtues nor vices are feelings: we are 'not called good or bad', or 'praised or blamed', on account of the latter, but 'we *are*' for the former, while virtues, but not feelings, are 'expressions of our choice' (p. 39). Virtues are not faculties: we are not 'praised or blamed' for being '*capable* of feeling', while nature gives us faculties, but nature does not make us 'good or bad' (p. 39). Thus, virtues are 'dispositions' (p. 39).

Book II

vi But what is its differentia? Any excellence enables its possessor to function well; therefore this is true of human excellence, i.e. virtue (pp. 39–41)

But what 'kind of disposition' is it (p. 39)? Any kind of excellence makes that of 'which it is the excellence *good*, and makes it perform its function *well*': the eye's excellence makes 'the eye and its function good', as through it 'we see well' (pp. 39–40). Similarly, '*human* excellence' will be the 'disposition' that makes someone 'a good man and causes him to perform his function well' (p. 40).

This is confirmed by the doctrine of the mean (pp. 40–1). With something that is 'continuous and divisible', there can be 'a part which is greater or less than, or equal to, the remainder': the third of these is a 'mean between excess and deficiency', which is 'the same for everybody' (p. 40). There is also a 'mean in relation to *us*' (p. 40). For example, if 'ten pounds' is a lot of food, and 'two pounds' a small amount, this does not mean a 'trainer' will prescribe six for a particular 'athlete': it might be 'too much or too little' for him (p. 40). 'Knowledgeable' people seek this second 'mean', which is 'relative' to them, and, if 'every science performs its function well only when it observes the mean', it follows that 'virtue aims to hit the mean' (pp. 40–1). I refer here to 'moral virtue', which concerns 'feelings and actions', as these involve 'excess, deficiency and a mean' (p. 41). It is possible, and wrong, to experience 'fear', 'anger', 'pleasure', and so on, 'too much or too little' (p. 41). The 'right way', and 'the mark of virtue', is to 'have these feelings' to an 'intermediate, that is to the best, degree'; and the same applies to 'actions' (p. 41). With both, 'excess and deficiency are failings', but 'the mean' is 'a success' (p. 41). Virtue 'aims at hitting the mean', but it is 'difficult to hit' this target (p. 41).

A provisional definition of virtue (p. 42). Virtue, then, is a 'purposive disposition, lying in a mean' between the two vices of 'excess' and 'deficiency', and which is 'relative to us and determined by a rational principle' (p. 42). In relation to both 'feelings and actions', the vices 'fall short of or exceed the right measure', but virtue 'chooses it' (p. 42) In its 'essence' it is 'a mean', but 'in respect of what is right and best, it is an extreme' (p. 42).

But the rule of choosing the mean cannot be applied to some actions and feelings, which are essentially evil (pp. 42–3). Feelings and actions, such as 'malice', 'envy', 'theft and murder', which are 'evil in themselves', do not admit of 'a mean' (p. 42). They are not evil through 'excess or deficiency': they are 'always wrong' (p. 42). Just as there is 'no mean or excess or deficiency' in 'temperance and courage', as 'the mean' here is 'an extreme', the same is true of these vices: excess and deficiency do not admit of a mean, nor does 'a mean admit of excess and deficiency' (pp. 42–3).

vii The doctrine of the mean applied to particular virtues (pp. 43–6)

But we must 'apply' all this 'to particular cases' (p. 43). With 'fear and confidence', 'courage' is the mean, and those with excessive or deficient 'confidence' are called 'rash' or 'cowardly' (p. 43). In relation to 'giving and receiving money', 'liberality' is the mean, and 'prodigality and illiberality' are the 'excess and deficiency' (43). With 'honour and dishonour', the 'mean is magnanimity', excess 'a sort of vanity', and deficiency **pusillanimity** (p. 44). One whose 'aspirations' go too far is 'ambitious', while one who 'falls short' in them is 'unambitious', but the mean 'has no name' (p. 44). Here, 'the extremes lay claim to the intermediate territory': the 'intermediate man' may sometimes be regarded as 'ambitious' or 'unambitious' (p. 44). In the 'field of anger', we may call 'the mean patience', while 'the extremes' are 'irascibility' and 'lack of spirit' (pp. 44–5).

There are means in 'social intercourse' (p. 45). With 'truth', the mean is 'truthfulness', and the extremes are 'boastfulness' and '**irony**' (p. 44). 'Pleasantness in social entertainment' is 'wit', the excess 'is **buffoonery**', and the deficiency '**boorishness**' (p. 45). In 'life in general', 'friendliness' is the mean, while one extreme is **obsequiousness** or flattery and the other is ill-temperedness (p. 45). 'Mean states' exist in 'the sphere of feelings' (p. 45). 'Modesty', though not a virtue, is praiseworthy, unlike the extremes of excessive shyness and shamelessness, while 'righteous indignation' is the mean between 'envy and spite', which concern 'feelings of pain or pleasure at the experiences of our neighbours' (pp. 45–6).

viii The mean is often nearer to one extreme than to the other, or seems nearer because of our natural tendencies (pp. 46–7)

The 'extremes' of 'excess' and 'deficiency' are 'contrary both to the mean and to each other, and the mean to the extremes' (p. 46). The 'mean states' are 'excessive compared with the deficient and deficient compared with the excessive', so a 'brave man' seems 'rash compared with a coward, and cowardly compared with a rash man'; but 'the greatest degree of contrariety' is between 'the two extremes' (pp. 46–7). However, either 'the deficiency' or 'the excess' may be 'more opposed to the mean': the 'direct opposite' of courage, for example, is 'cowardice' (the deficiency), not 'rashness' (the excess) (p. 47). Thus, we 'tend to oppose to the mean' the 'extreme' that is further from it: we oppose cowardice to courage, as being 'more opposed to it' (p. 47). We also view the 'things towards which we have the stronger natural inclination' as 'more opposed to the mean': we are 'inclined towards pleasures', and so regard 'licentiousness' as being 'contrary to temperance' (p. 47).

ix Summing-up of the foregoing discussion, together with three practical rules for good conduct (pp. 48–9)

So, 'moral virtue' is a 'mean' that aims at 'hitting the mean point in feelings and actions'; and this is difficult to do (p. 48). It is easy to 'get angry', or to 'give and spend money', but not to 'feel or act towards the right person to the right extent at the right time for the right reason in the right way' (p. 48). In particular, (1) we need to avoid the extreme that is 'more contrary to the mean', for one is 'always more erroneous than the other', and 'choose the lesser of the evils'; (2) we must be aware of our own common 'errors', and 'drag ourselves in the contrary direction'; and (3) we must be vigilant about 'pleasure and pleasant things', because we are not 'impartial judges' of them (pp. 48–9). Following 'these rules' gives us the 'best chance of hitting the mean', although it is not easy (p. 49). For example, what is 'the right way to be angry' (p. 49)? We sometimes commend 'deficiency' as patience, and a 'display' of temper as manliness (p. 49). Normally, censure is not applied to small deviations from 'the right degree', but it is hard to specify 'how long, and how much, a man may go wrong before he incurs blame' (p. 49).

Book III

Moral Responsibility: Two Virtues (pp. 50–81)

*i Actions are voluntary, involuntary or non-voluntary
(pp. 50–4)*

As 'voluntary' actions are praised or blamed, while 'involuntary' ones are pardoned, 'students of moral goodness' must 'determine the limits of the voluntary and involuntary' (p. 50). Involuntary ones are the result of 'compulsion' (they have an 'external origin', to which the agent 'contributes nothing') or 'ignorance' (p. 50). However, the dividing-line between the two groups is not clear-cut. For example, a tyrant might require someone 'to do something dishonourable' on threat of harming his 'parents and children' (p. 50). Such actions are 'mixed' (p. 50). When performing them 'the agent acts voluntarily' in that he has the 'power either to act or not', yet 'nobody would choose to do anything of this sort in itself' (p. 51). Again, there are some things a person 'cannot be compelled to do', which 'he must sooner die than do'; and 'agents are praised or blamed according to whether they have yielded to compulsion or not' (p. 51).

What 'sort of acts' should we regard as compulsory (p. 51)? Strictly, those where 'the cause is external' and the 'agent contributes nothing' (p. 51). Acts that originate 'in the agent', though 'involuntary in themselves', are 'voluntary at the given time and cost' (pp. 51–2). The contention that 'pleasurable and admirable things' have 'a compulsive effect' would make 'all acts compulsory', as it is for such objects that every act is done (p. 52). Further, the agent cannot blame external factors when he falls 'an easy prey to them', and attributes 'fine acts to himself' and 'disgraceful ones' to pleasure (p. 52). An act done 'through ignorance' is 'non-voluntary', provided the agent feels 'pain and repentance' (p. 52). Also, acting *'through'* and *'in* ignorance' must be distinguished (p. 52). It is not 'ignorance in the choice' (a 'cause of wickedness'), or ignorance of the moral principle (people are 'blamed' for this), but *'particular* ignorance' ('of the circumstances') that makes an act 'involuntary' (p. 53). These circumstances relate to (1) the 'agent' (but he 'cannot be ignorant' of himself); (2) the 'act' (the agent may not realize 'what he is doing'); (3) the 'object or medium of the act' (he might be mistaken about his 'enemy'); (4) the 'instrument' (he might think 'a sharp-pointed spear had a button on it'); (5) 'the aim' (he might 'kill someone' with what was intended as a life-saving drug); (6) 'the manner': 'gently or roughly' (he might hit someone when he only meant to 'seize his hand') (p. 53). Anyone who is ignorant of such 'particular circumstances' is deemed to 'have acted involuntarily', as long as he feels 'distress and repentance' (pp. 53–4).

Voluntary acts are ones where 'the originating cause lies in the agent himself', who is aware of all the circumstances (p. 54). We must not try to say that only our 'discreditable' actions are done 'involuntarily', as this would be 'absurd', and it is also wrong to call 'acts to which we are rightly attracted' involuntary (p. 54). There are things that should make us 'angry', and others, such as 'health' and 'learning', that we 'ought to desire' (p. 54). No distinction can be made 'in point of voluntariness' between 'wrong actions that are calculated' and those 'due to temper' (we must avoid both): 'irrational feelings' belong to 'human nature' as much as 'considered judgements' (p. 54).

ii Moral conduct implies choice, but what is choice? It must be distinguished from desire, temper, wish and opinion (pp. 54–6)

Choice and 'moral goodness' are 'very closely related', and the former is 'clearly a voluntary thing'; but not all voluntary actions involve choice (pp. 54–5). It is wrong to 'identify it with desire', as 'a desire can be contrary to choice', while desire, but not choice, concerns 'what is pleasurable and painful' (p. 55). Again, one can 'wish for what is impossible', such as 'immortality', but there is 'no choice of impossibilities', while one can 'wish for results' that one cannot 'bring about oneself', but 'nobody *chooses*' them (p. 55). Wish is 'more concerned with the end', choice 'with the means': we say we 'wish to be happy', but not that 'we choose to be' (p. 55). As for opinions, they are 'true or false', not 'good or bad' like choices: choice is about 'choosing the right object', rather than 'being correct in itself' (p. 56). Further, some who are 'good at forming opinions' do not 'make the right choices', as a result of 'moral defect' (p. 56).

So, what is the 'specific quality' of choice (p. 56)? It is 'the result of previous deliberation', for it 'implies a rational principle, and thought' (p. 56).

iii If choice involves deliberation, what is the sphere of the latter? (pp. 57–9)

Do we 'deliberate about all issues' (p. 57)? Not, it seems, about some things, such as 'eternal facts' like 'the order of the universe', or about 'regular processes' (whether they have 'a necessary or a natural' cause), such as 'the risings of the sun' (p. 57). The subjects of deliberation are 'practical measures that lie in our power', and which concern us (p. 57). We deliberate about 'the effects' that are 'produced by our agency', as in 'medicine', 'finance' and 'navigation' (p. 57). The 'arts call for more deliberation than the sciences', as we are 'less certain about them' (p. 58). Generally, we deliberate about things where 'the right course' is 'not clearly defined' (p. 58).

Deliberation is about means, not ends (pp. 58–9). Deliberation is about 'means' (p. 58). A statesman, for example, does not deliberate about 'whether to produce law and order', nor does a doctor about 'whether to cure his patient' (p. 58). They set 'some end', and then consider 'how and by what means it can be attained' (p. 58). As long as 'the thing appears possible' (by which I mean that it 'can be done by our agency'), they then 'set about doing it' (p. 58).

So, 'the originating cause of actions is a man', and deliberation relates to 'what is practicable for the agent', whose 'object' is 'the means to ends' (p. 59). The objects of 'deliberation' and 'choice are the same', but the latter has 'already been determined', as 'the result' of the former (p. 59). A 'man stops inquiring how to act when he has traced the starting-point of action back to himself': that is, to the 'dominant part' that 'makes the choice' (p. 59).

Definition of choice (p. 59). Choice then is 'a deliberate **appetition** of things that lie in our power'. After deciding, 'as the result of deliberation', we 'direct our aim' accordingly.

iv The object of wish is in one sense the good, in another the apparent good (p. 60)

Wishing is concerned with 'the end', and some think 'its object is the good', others 'the *apparent* good' (p. 60). For those of the first view, a person choosing 'wrongly' means that what he wishes is not 'an object of wish', because, to be 'wishable', it 'must be good' (p. 60). For those of the second view, nothing is 'by nature wishable'; rather, what 'any individual' considers good is 'wishable for him' (p. 60).

Perhaps, we should say that the 'object of wish' is 'the good', but, 'for the individual', it is what 'seems good' to him (p. 60). For the 'man of good character', this will be 'the true good', but will be 'any chance thing' for the 'bad man' (p. 60). The former 'judges every situation rightly', and 'what appears to him is the truth'; he is a 'standard' of 'what is fine and pleasant' (p. 60). Many are deceived by 'pleasure' which 'appears to them to be good', and so they choose it as 'good', shunning 'pain as an evil' (p. 60).

v Actions that we initiate ourselves, whether they are good or bad, are voluntary (p. 61)

The end is 'an object of wish', and the means 'objects of deliberation and choice', so actions relating to the latter will be done 'voluntarily' (p. 61). As 'the exercise of moral virtues' relates to the means, both virtue and vice are 'in our power': we can do what is right, and not do what is wrong; and, as this is 'the essence of being good or bad', we decide whether to be 'decent or worthless' (p. 61). Clearly, if we are the begetters of our 'own actions', as of our own 'children', their origin lies in ourselves and is 'in our power' (p. 61).

This is borne out by the common use of rewards and punishments (p. 62). The use of 'honours' to reward 'fine actions', and of penalties to punish 'malefactors' (unless 'the offence' was 'committed under duress or in unavoidable ignorance') supports 'this view', as their object seems to be to encourage the former and restrain the latter (p. 62).

Responsibility for the results of bad moral states (p. 62). People are punished for 'ignorance', if they are 'responsible for it'

(p. 62). A drunken person who commits a crime was 'capable of not getting drunk', while ignorance of points of law, which should be known, is punished (p. 62). The cause is 'the slackness' of people's lives: their moral state is 'the result' of how they live (pp. 62–3). They 'develop qualities' that correspond to their 'activities', making themselves 'unjust or **licentious**', through dishonesty or drinking (pp. 62–3).

A bad moral state, once formed, is not easily amended (p. 63). It is 'unreasonable' to think that one who 'acts unjustly or licentiously' does not do so 'voluntarily', but this does not mean he can stop, 'if he wants to', any more than 'a sick man' can 'become healthy', even if his illness results from 'incontinent living' (p. 63). It was in the power of 'unjust and licentious persons' not to 'become such' in the first place, but, having become so, 'it is no longer open to them not to be' (p. 63).

Even physical defects, if voluntarily incurred, are culpable (pp. 63–4). Even 'physical defects' can be 'voluntarily incurred', as when people fail to take exercise, and we 'blame them for it' (p. 63). We pity a person 'blind by nature', but condemn one who has caused his blindness by 'heavy drinking' (p. 64). Similarly, with 'moral defects', it is the ones we are responsible for 'that are blamed' (p. 64).

It may be objected that moral discernment is a gift of nature and cannot be acquired otherwise (p. 64). Some argue that everybody aims at 'what appears to him to be good', but does not control this, as it depends on 'his character': that, if he is not 'responsible for his moral state', he is not responsible for his 'view of what is good'; or, therefore, for what he does wrong (p. 64). One with a 'good natural disposition' (they contend) has the advantage of what cannot be 'had or learnt from another': an inborn ability 'to judge correctly and choose what is truly good' (p. 64).

Even so, virtue will be no more voluntary than vice (p. 65). On this argument, how can 'virtue be more voluntary than vice' (p. 65)? Whether (1) the 'individual's view of the end' depends at least 'partly on himself', or (2) 'is the gift of nature', 'virtue is voluntary', because the 'good man performs voluntarily all the means towards the end' (p. 65). Vice is 'no less voluntary', because 'the bad man has just as much independence in his *actions*, even if not in his choice of the end', as the good man (p. 65).

So, virtues are 'mean states and dispositions' that are 'voluntary', and which 'enable their possessor to perform the same sort of actions as those by which they are acquired', and to 'act as the 'right principle prescribes' (p. 65). However, our actions and dispositions are not 'voluntary in the same sense': we control the former from 'beginning to end', the latter only at 'the beginning' (p. 65).

Now to discuss the virtues one by one (p. 66). We will now explain what each virtue is 'one by one' (p. 66).

vi Courage: the right attitude towards feelings of fear and confidence. What we ought and ought not to fear (pp. 66–7)

We know courage is 'a mean state in relation to feelings of fear and confidence' (p. 66). We 'fear all evils', such as 'poverty, sickness' and 'death', but they do not all concern 'the courageous man', as there are some, such as 'disgrace', which the 'upright and decent' man should fear (p. 66). Probably, one should not fear anything (for example, 'poverty or disease') that does not result from 'vice or one's own fault' (p. 66). Again, one is not cowardly for dreading 'brutality towards his wife and children' (pp. 66–7).

What 'terrors' concern the 'courageous man' (p. 67)? The

'most fearful thing' is death, but not all types offer 'scope for courage' (p. 67). The 'noblest' form of death is in warfare, where, as the 'honours paid to the fallen' show, the 'danger is greatest and most glorious' (p. 67). The 'courageous man' is thus one who is 'fearless in the face of an honourable death', or a 'sudden' one; and these occur mainly 'in war' (p. 67). Courage can also be shown 'in situations that give scope for stout resistance or a glorious death' (p. 67).

vii Degrees of fear and fearfulness (pp. 67–8)

We do not all find the same things 'terrible' (p. 67). Some things are said to be 'beyond human endurance', but they differ in the degree of 'fear that they inspire' (p. 67). The courageous man is 'undaunted', as far as is 'humanly possible', fearing what man naturally fears, but facing it 'in the right way', for 'the sake of what is right and honourable', as this is 'the end of virtue' (pp. 67–8). It is possible to fear 'the wrong thing', but the courageous man fears 'the right things for the right reason and in the right way and at the right time' (p. 68). His courage is 'a noble thing', and he faces dangers 'for a right and noble motive', performing actions 'appropriate to his courage' (p. 68).

Excessive fearlessness, rashness and cowardice (pp. 68–9). One who is 'afraid of nothing' is 'a maniac or insensate' (p. 68). The 'rash man' is seen as wishing to '*seem* as the courageous man really *is* in his attitude towards fearful situations': he makes a 'show of confidence' (pp. 68–9). The excessively fearful man is 'a coward', fearing 'the wrong things in the wrong way' (p. 69). He is also 'despondent', but 'the opposite' is true of the courageous man who shows 'confidence', which is the 'mark of optimism' (p. 69). The rash man and the coward show 'excess and deficiency', but the courageous man has 'the right disposition and observes the mean' (p. 69).

Courage is 'a mean state', relating to 'things conducive to confidence or fear', which 'faces danger' as a 'fine thing to do' (p. 69). Killing oneself is cowardly, because it involves running away 'from hardships', and enduring death only to 'escape from suffering' (p. 69).

viii Five dispositions that resemble courage (pp. 70–3)

(1) Civic courage (pp. 70–1)

This is considered 'very like courage proper', because 'citizens' face dangers, due to 'the honours' (p. 70). Its 'ground is a moral virtue': 'a desire for something noble' and 'avoidance of reproach' (p. 70). Those ordered to 'face death by their commanders' are 'inferior', as they do so 'through fear', not 'shame': one should be 'brave not under compulsion but because it is a fine thing' (pp. 70–1).

(2) Experience of risk (pp. 71–2)

Experiencing certain sorts of 'risk', as soldiers do in war, is 'regarded as a form of courage' (p. 71). Of course, 'many false alarms' occur in war; experienced soldiers know this, and are able to make themselves 'appear to be brave' (p. 71). Again, the 'best fighters' may not be 'the bravest', but the 'strongest and fittest physically' (p. 71). When 'danger is extreme', it may be the 'professional soldiers' who run away, while 'the citizen troops die at their posts' (p. 71). Unlike the latter, the former 'fear death more than dishonour', but this is not the courageous man's view (pp. 71–2).

(3) *Spirit or mettle (p. 72)*

'Spirit' is also regarded as courage, as it is 'very bold in the face of danger' (p. 72). However, while 'courageous people act for a fine motive', and 'their spirit' is a mere 'accessory', 'beasts' are not courageous just because, 'impelled by pain and anger', they 'rush into danger, blind to the risks' (p. 72). 'The quasi-courage', 'due to spirit', is regarded as courage if it 'includes deliberate choice', but those who fight, as a result of pain and anger, are not acting 'from a fine motive' or 'on principle', but 'from feeling' (p. 72).

(4) *Sanguineness or optimism (p. 73)*

Although they are 'confident', 'sanguine people' are not courageous: they just regard themselves as 'the best soldiers', who 'cannot lose'; and, when things do not 'turn out as expected', they run away (p. 73). However, the courageous man faces up to 'terrible' things, because it is 'a fine act' to do so (p. 73). Thus, it is thought 'better proof of courage' to remain 'undismayed' in the face of 'sudden', rather than 'foreseen', alarms: it arises 'more directly from the moral state', because no 'preparation' is involved (p. 73).

(5) *Ignorance (p. 73)*

Those acting 'in ignorance' only 'appear to be courageous': if they discover that things are not as they supposed, they 'run away', as 'the **Argives' did when they thought 'the Spartans' were 'Sicyonians'** (p. 73).

ix Courage in relation to pleasure and pain (pp. 74–5)

Courage concerns 'grounds for confidence and fear', but the latter to a greater extent (p. 74). It 'implies the presence of pain', and should be 'praised', as 'it is harder to bear pain' than 'abstain from pleasure' (p. 74). The 'end of an act' involving courage may be pleasant, but the 'attendant circumstances' obscure this (p. 74). However, 'the courageous man' endures 'death and wounds', as it is 'the fine thing to do' (p. 74). Death is very distressing to the virtuous man, because his 'life is supremely worth living'; but this probably makes him 'even braver' (p. 74). Of course, 'professional soldiers' may be 'less brave', but, having only their lives to lose, are prepared to 'sell' them 'for petty gains' (pp. 74–5).

x Temperance or self-control, and the pleasures with which it is concerned (pp. 75–7)

Like courage, 'temperance', a 'mean state with regard to pleasures', is a virtue thought to 'belong to the **irrational parts of the soul**' (p. 75). What 'kind of pleasures' (p. 75)?

Pleasures are either psychical or physical (pp. 75–6). There are pleasures 'of the soul', such as love of '**civic distinction**' and 'learning', and those of 'the body'; and those who enjoy the former are not termed either 'temperate' or 'licentious' (p. 75). So, temperance concerns bodily pleasures, but not those involving 'objects of sight' or 'hearing' (p. 76). With those 'who enjoy smells', we describe as 'licentious' only those 'who do so by association', as when people enjoy the smell of such things as 'perfume and savoury dishes', which remind them of 'the objects of their desires' (p. 76). Animals also experience 'pleasure through their senses' only 'by association': hounds do not enjoy 'the smell of hares', but 'the eating of them' (p. 76).

The grossest pleasures are those of taste and, above all, touch (p. 77). So, 'temperance and licentiousness' concern the 'low and brutish' pleasures of 'touch and taste', which are 'shared by animals' (p. 77). And, for the 'licentious person', it is not really 'the flavours that gratify', but 'enjoyment', which, whether in food and drink or sex, 'depends entirely upon touch' (p. 77). This sense 'attaches to us not as men but as animals', so to 'find the greatest satisfaction' in 'such sensations' is 'brutish' (p. 77).

xi Desires or appetites; self-indulgence and insensibility (pp. 77–9)

'Desires' seem to be either 'general or particular' (p. 77). Desire for food 'is natural', as everyone 'needs' it, as they do 'sexual intercourse' when 'young and lusty' (pp. 77–8). But, as not everyone desires a 'particular kind of food or sex', appetite, although it has a 'natural element' (some things are 'more than averagely pleasing to everyone'), seems 'a matter of personal taste' (p. 78). With 'natural desires', few go wrong, except 'in the direction of too much': the natural desire is just for 'replenishment of the deficiency' (p. 78). But, with 'particular pleasures', people err in enjoying 'the wrong objects', or enjoying things with 'abnormal intensity'; and 'the licentious display excess in every form' (p. 78).

Unlike courage, a man is not called 'temperate' for enduring pain, and 'licentious' for not doing so (p. 78). The latter type 'desires all pleasant things', and his desire leads him to choose them 'before anything else' (p. 78). He 'feels pain', both when failing to get them and when desiring them, and it is 'preposterous to feel pain on account of pleasure' (p. 78). In relation to pleasures, 'deficiency' (desiring them 'less than one ought') rarely occurs: a person like this would be 'very far from being human' (pp. 78–9).

The temperate man does not enjoy the things 'the licentious man enjoys most' or 'wrong pleasures', and is not distressed by 'absence of pleasures' (p. 79). He holds a 'mean position', pursuing, 'in moderation', pleasures conducive to 'health' and those that are not 'dishonourable or beyond his means', and appreciating them as 'the right principle directs' (p. 79).

xii *Licentiousness is more voluntary than cowardice* (pp. 79–80)

Licentiousness is 'more like a voluntary thing' than cowardice, because pain, which the coward seeks to avoid, 'distracts the sufferer and impairs his natural state', whereas pleasure, which the licentious person chooses, does not have this 'effect' (p. 79). One can 'train oneself to resist pleasures', and this involves 'no danger' (p. 79). Indeed, 'particular instances' of cowardice are seen as 'compulsive', as pain can so distract a person that he 'throws away his weapons' and 'disgraces himself' (p. 80). While no one may desire to be licentious, the 'licentious man' performs 'particular acts' from 'desire and appetite' (p. 80).

Licentious people are like spoilt children (pp. 80–1). The 'faults of children' are also named 'licentiousness', and this is appropriate, as 'restraint' is needed for those with 'low appetites and a marked capacity for growth', as is the case with children and desires (p. 80). Children are impelled by their desires, and similarly, in an 'irrational being', the appetite for what gives pleasure is 'insatiable and indiscriminate', while exercising it increases its 'innate tendency' and can 'drive out reason' (p. 80). So, just as the child must submit to his tutor's 'directions', the 'rational principle' should control our 'desiderative element' (pp. 80–1). The latter needs to be 'in harmony with' the former, both having as their object 'attainment of what is admirable': the 'temperate man' desires 'the right things in the right way and at the right time' (p. 81).

Book VI

Intellectual Virtues (pp. 144–66)

i *What is the right principle that should regulate conduct?* (pp. 144–5)

We say the 'mean' is 'as the right principle dictates' (p. 144). In all 'the states', described above, there is 'a sort of target', and one with this 'principle' has 'his eyes' on it; there is also 'a sort of limit' that determines the 'mean states' between 'excess and deficiency' (p. 144). But to say one should 'exert oneself' or 'relax' to a 'mean extent' is not very 'explicit': we need to know 'what the right principle is' (p. 144).

Contemplative and calculative intellect (p. 145). In our classification of 'the virtues of the soul', we said some were of 'character', 'others of the intellect' (p. 145). Having discussed 'moral virtues', we shall now look at 'the remainder' (p. 145).

We have stated that the soul has a 'rational' and an 'irrational' part (p. 145). This is also the case with the rational part: it has a part to 'contemplate' things with 'invariable' first principles, and another for 'variable' ones; and these, the 'scientific' and 'calculative' parts (nobody calculates or 'deliberates' about invariable things), are 'themselves different in kind' (p. 145). We need to understand 'the best state' of both of them, as that will be 'the virtue of each' (p. 145).

*ii Both kinds of intellect aim at truth, but the calculative
faculty aims at truth as rightly desired by the exercise of choice
(pp. 146–7)*

A thing's 'virtue' relates to 'its proper function' (p. 146). Three
things in the soul, 'sensation, intellect and appetition', control
'action and the attainment of truth', of which the first is not
'the origin of any action' (p. 146). Since 'moral virtue' involves
choice, which is 'deliberate appetition', for choice to be good,
the 'reasoning must be true and the desire right' (p. 146).
We refer here to 'intellect and truth in a practical sense': the
'function of practical intellect' is to reach 'the truth that corresponds to right appetition' (p. 146).

The **'efficient' cause** of action is 'choice', which originates
in 'appetition and purposive reasoning' (p. 146). It involves
'a certain moral state', for 'good conduct' necessarily involves
both 'thought and character', as nothing is 'set going by mere
thought', but only by 'practical thought' (p. 146). Thus, choice
is either 'appetitive intellect or intellectual appetition' (p. 147).
Attaining truth is 'the task of both of the intellectual parts of
the soul', and their 'respective virtues are the states that will
best enable them to arrive at the truth' (p. 147).

*iii Five modes of thought or states of mind by which truth is
reached (pp. 147–8)*

There are 'five ways' that 'the soul arrives at truth by affirmation or denial': '**art**, **science**, **prudence**, **wisdom** and **intuition**';
as '**judgement** and **opinion**' are liable to be 'mistaken', they are
left out (p. 147).

Science or scientific knowledge (p. 148). We assume that 'what
we *know* cannot be otherwise than it is', so the 'object of scientific knowledge' is 'necessity', and this is 'eternal': it cannot

'come into being or cease to be' (p. 148). 'Scientific knowledge' is 'teachable', and this begins from what is 'already known', as it proceeds either by **'induction'** (which 'introduces us to first principles and universals') or **'deduction'** (which 'starts from universals': they are 'not deducible', and are 'reached by induction') (p. 148). It is a **'demonstrative** state': someone has scientific knowledge when he knows 'the first principles' (p. 148). If he does not know them better 'than the conclusion drawn from them', he will have 'knowledge only incidentally' (p. 148).

iv Art or technical skill (p. 149)

The 'class of variables' comprises both 'products and acts', but 'production' and 'action' are different (p. 149). 'Building is an art' and a 'reasoned productive state'; thus, art is a 'productive state that is truly reasoned', concerned with 'bringing something into being', which has, as its 'cause', 'the producer'; and, as production and action are 'not the same', art must be concerned with the former (p. 149).

v Prudence or practical wisdom (pp. 150–1)

We can understand this by considering the kind of people 'we call prudent': they are able 'to deliberate rightly' about 'what is conducive to the good life generally', so a prudent man is one 'capable of deliberation' (p. 150). However, as scientific knowledge 'implies the ability to demonstrate'; as 'variable' things (those that 'may actually be otherwise') cannot be demonstrated; and as it is 'impossible to deliberate about things that are *necessarily* so', prudence is not 'science', because it concerns what is 'variable', while it is 'not art', because 'action and production' are 'generically different' (p. 150). The latter 'aims at an end other than itself', while action is 'merely doing *well*' (p. 150). Thus, prudence is a 'reasoned' state, 'capable of action' in relation to things that are 'good or bad for man': people like **Pericles**, who can see 'what is good' for themselves and others, are prudent (p. 150). We apply the term to 'temperance', as it 'preserves wisdom' (pp. 150–1).

Thus, prudence is a 'true state, reasoned and capable of action in the sphere of human goods' (p. 151). It is a virtue of that part of the soul that 'forms opinions', because both it and opinion concern 'the variable' (p. 151).

vi Intelligence or intuition (pp. 151–2)

Scientific knowledge is 'forming judgements' about 'universal and necessary' things, and it depends on 'first principles' (pp. 151–2). Thus, the 'first principles of scientific truths' cannot be 'grasped' by science, art or prudence, for 'scientific truth is demonstrable', and art and prudence are to do with 'the variable' (p. 152). The 'first principles' are not the sole concern of 'wisdom', because 'the wise man' is able to '*demonstrate* some things' (p. 152). If the 'states of mind' by which we 'reach the truth' in relation to 'variable and invariable' things are 'science, prudence, wisdom and intuition', and the one that 'apprehends first principles' cannot be among the first three, it must be 'intuition' (p. 152).

vii Wisdom (pp. 152–4)

We use the term 'wisdom' of the 'most finished experts in the arts', which just indicates 'excellence' in that field (p. 152). But some are 'wise without qualification', so it is 'the most finished form of knowledge' (p. 152). Thus, the wise man both knows and understands 'the first principles' and 'all that follows' from them, so wisdom is 'intuition *and* scientific knowledge' (pp. 152–3). It is not the same as prudence, for even 'brutes', who can 'provide for their own survival', are regarded as 'prudent' (p. 153). It is not the same as 'political science', either, for if people described as 'wisdom' what is 'beneficial to themselves', there would be 'more than one' type (p. 153). So, wisdom is 'scientific and intuitive knowledge' of that which is 'by nature most precious' (p. 153). Men like '**Anaxagoras** and **Thales**' are called 'wise', but not 'prudent', because they seem 'ignorant of their own advantage' (p. 153). Prudence concerns 'human goods', about which there can be 'deliberation' (p. 154). Nobody deliberates about things 'that cannot be otherwise', and that are not the 'means to an end', which is a 'practical good'; and one who excels in deliberation is able, by its means, to aim at 'the best of the goods attainable by man' (p. 154).

Further, prudence is to do with 'conduct', which requires knowledge of 'particular circumstances', rather than 'universals' (p. 154). Often, those who lack 'theoretical knowledge' are 'more effective in action' (p. 154). For example, one who knows that 'chicken is wholesome', is more likely to be healthy than one who knows that 'light flesh foods' are 'wholesome', but does not know which they are (p. 154). Prudence is 'practical', and needs 'both kinds of knowledge', but 'especially the former' (p. 154).

viii The political sciences are species of prudence (pp. 154–7)

Political science and prudence are 'the same state of mind' (p. 154). There are 'two aspects' to 'prudence concerning the state': 'legislative science' ('controlling and directive'), and 'political science' (dealing with 'particular circumstances'), which is 'practical and deliberative' (p. 154). Prudence is especially concerned with 'the self', and it is of this 'form' of prudence that the term itself is used; the other forms are 'domestic, legislative and political science' (p. 155). Knowledge of 'one's own interests' is a 'species of knowledge' that differs from others, and those who limit themselves to these, and 'seek their own good', are considered 'prudent', while 'politicians' are thought to be 'busybodies' (p. 155). However, 'it is impossible to secure one's own good independently of domestic and political science' (p. 155).

Young people may 'develop ability' in such fields as 'geometry and mathematics', but are not considered prudent, as this requires 'knowledge of particular facts', which must be gained 'from experience' (pp. 155–6). This explains why they can be mathematicians (dealing with 'abstractions'), but not philosophers or natural scientists, as these subjects can be 'grasped only as the result of experience' (p. 156).

Prudence contrasted with science and intuition (pp. 156–7). Prudence is 'opposite to intuition': the second 'apprehends the definitions, which cannot be logically demonstrated', while the first 'apprehends the ultimate particular, which cannot be apprehended by scientific knowledge' (pp. 156–7).

ix Resourcefulness or good deliberation distinguished from other intellectual qualities (pp. 157–9)

Resourcefulness, which is a 'kind of deliberation', is not 'knowledge', because people do not 'inquire about' things they know; it is not 'conjecture', which is 'rapid', as deliberation is a slow process; and it is not 'readiness of mind', or 'any kind of opinion' either (p. 157). It is a 'species of correctness', as one who 'deliberates well' does so 'correctly', but not of knowledge, where there is no 'error', or of 'opinion', the object of which 'is already determined' (p. 157). What remains is that it is 'correctness of thinking'; and as one who deliberates is 'inquiring into something', it is a 'species of correctness of deliberation' (p. 158).

'Correctness' has more than one use (p. 158). A 'wicked person' can deliberate correctly, and achieve 'something very detrimental', but the result of 'correctness in deliberation' (the sort that 'constitutes resourcefulness') is thought to be 'something good' (p. 158). Again, it is possible to achieve 'the right end' by the wrong means, while someone may succeed after quick, as well as long, deliberation, so all this 'falls short of resourcefulness, which is correctness in estimating advantage with respect to the right object, the right means and the right time' (p. 158).

x Understanding (pp. 159–60)

This is not the same as 'scientific knowledge or opinion', for then everyone would have it; and it is not a particular science, like 'medicine' or 'geometry' (p. 159). It is not concerned with 'eternal and immutable' things, nor those that come 'into being', but with 'matters' causing perplexity and requiring 'deliberation' (p. 159). Its 'sphere is the same' as prudence, but the latter is 'imperative' (its end is 'what one should or should not do'), while 'understanding only makes judgements' (p. 159). It is not having or acquiring prudence; but in 'exercising the faculty of opinion', to judge another's 'account of matters within the scope of prudence', the 'act of judging' (rightly) is 'called understanding' (p. 159).

Book VI

xi Judgement and consideration (pp. 160–1)

This is 'the faculty of judging correctly what is equitable': it is commonly held that the 'equitable man' is 'sympathetic in his judgements', and that, in 'certain circumstances', it is 'equitable to judge sympathetically' (p. 160). The latter is a 'correct judgement' (one that 'arrives at the truth') that 'decides what is equitable' (p. 160).

General comments on the various states of mind (pp. 160–1). These 'states of mind naturally tend to coalesce', as 'judgement, understanding, prudence', and so on are attributed 'to the same persons' (p. 160). To be 'understanding' and 'sympathetic' is to be 'able to judge' about matters that concern 'the prudent man': 'equitable acts are common to all good men in their behaviour towards others' (pp. 160–1).

Although a person may have 'judgement and understanding and intuition', nobody is thought to be 'endowed by nature with wisdom' (p. 161). We should heed the 'unproved assertions and opinions of experienced and older people [or of prudent people]' as much as 'demonstrations of fact', as they have 'insight' as a result of 'their experience' (p. 161).

xii The value of the intellectual virtues (pp. 162–3)

What is 'the use' of 'the intellectual virtues' (p. 162)? Wisdom does not deal with things that 'make a man happy'; prudence is concerned with just acts, which are 'good for man', but '*knowing* about them' does not enable us to do them (p. 162). Again, if prudence's use is 'with a view to becoming good', this does not help those 'who are good already' (p. 162). Further, it could seem 'paradoxical' that prudence, which is 'inferior to wisdom', should be 'more authoritative' (p. 162).

We shall say that 'wisdom and prudence' are both 'virtues'

(each of 'one part of the soul'), and are 'desirable in themselves' (pp. 162–3). Wisdom 'produces happiness', as it is 'part of virtue as a whole', making people happy by possessing and exercising it (p. 163). Again, 'full performance of a man's function' depends on 'prudence and moral virtue' together: the second ensures 'the correctness' of our end, the former 'the means towards it' (p. 163). Moreover, we must look again at our view that 'prudence does not make us any more capable of doing fine and just acts' (p. 163). We say that some of those who 'perform just acts are still not just', but there appears to be 'a state of mind' in which someone can do things 'in such a way as to be a good man' (p. 163). Virtue makes 'the choice correct', but 'carrying out' all the 'stages of action' to reach that 'chosen end' is a matter for 'a different faculty' (p. 163).

A new factor: the faculty of cleverness (p. 164). The faculty 'called cleverness' can carry out actions, 'conducive to' achieving 'our proposed aim', and so is 'praiseworthy' if the aim is 'noble', but 'unscrupulous' if it is 'ignoble' (p. 164). It is implied by, but 'not identical with', prudence, which 'the insight of the soul' cannot reach 'without virtue' (p. 164). 'Practical syllogisms' always begin: 'Since the end or supreme good is such-and-such'; and only 'a good man' can see this, as 'wickedness distorts the vision' (p. 164). So, one 'cannot be prudent without being good' (p. 164).

xiii How prudence is related to natural virtue and virtue proper (pp. 164–6)

'Natural' virtue's relation to 'virtue in the true sense' is rather like that of 'prudence' to 'cleverness' (p. 164). Although it is generally believed that the 'various kinds of character' are 'gifts of nature', we 'expect to find' that 'moral qualities are acquired in another way', as 'natural dispositions' (found also, 'without intelligence', in children and animals) are 'apt to be harmful' (pp. 164–5). It is when someone 'acquires intelligence' that his conduct becomes 'outstanding', and 'his disposition', instead of just *resembling* it, is 'virtue in the full sense'; and it is this that 'implies prudence' (p. 165).

Many people, including **Socrates**, have thought that 'all the virtues are forms of prudence'; and when we define 'virtue', we 'add the qualification "in accordance with the right principle"', and this is what 'accords with prudence' (p. 165). Indeed, 'the right principle in moral conduct is prudence' (pp. 165–6). So, though not (as Socrates thought) 'principles', the virtues do '*imply*' one, and it is possible neither to be good 'without prudence', nor prudent 'without moral goodness' (p. 166). It has been argued that virtues 'exist independently of each other', and that a man can possess one without another (p. 166). However, having 'the single virtue of prudence' brings with it 'possession of them all' (p. 166). Correct choice cannot be made without 'goodness', which 'identifies the end', or 'prudence', which leads us to 'perform the acts that are means towards it' (p. 166). But prudence does not have 'authority' over wisdom or the 'higher part of the soul': it does not give 'orders' to wisdom, but 'for its sake' (p. 166).

Book X

Pleasure and the Life of Happiness (pp. 254–84)

i The importance of pleasure in ethics, and the conflict of views about its value (pp. 254–5)

Pleasure is very important in 'forming' the 'character to like or dislike the right things': it permeates 'the whole of life', powerfully influencing 'virtue and the happy life', as people choose the pleasant and avoid pain (p. 254). Some hold that 'pleasure is the good', others that it is 'wholly bad' (p. 254). Some of the latter really think it is so, but others, believing human beings are 'slaves of their self-indulgence', think we 'need to be urged in the opposite direction', in order to 'attain to the mean' (p. 254). However, 'theories' that are at odds with what 'our senses' tell us damage 'the cause of truth', and, if those who denounce pleasure are seen to be 'drawn towards it', this is taken to suggest that they regard 'all pleasure as desirable' (p. 255). 'True theories' help us to live our lives well, because they agree 'with the facts', and so 'encourage those who understand them to live under their direction' (p. 255).

ii Eudoxus' view, that pleasure is the supreme good, is not above dispute (pp. 255–6)

Eudoxus, seeing that both 'rational and irrational' creatures are 'attracted' to it, thought that: 'pleasure is the good'; that, 'in every case what is desirable is good'; and that 'what is most desirable is best' (p. 255). All creatures being drawn to it shows (he believed) that it is 'best for all', as 'each individual' seeks 'its own good'; and what is 'good for all', 'which all try to obtain, is the good' (p. 255). His 'excellence' of character lent weight to his argument: he was regarded as 'self-controlled' and not a mere 'pleasure-lover' (p. 255). He thought that people's attitude to 'pain', which is 'shunned by all', supported his view, and maintained that the 'most desirable thing' is that which is never chosen 'as a means to' something else: nobody is asked '*why* he is enjoying himself', as pleasure is considered 'desirable in itself' (pp. 255–6).

He also contended that adding pleasure to something good,

such as 'temperate conduct', makes it 'more desirable' (p. 256). But this suggests that pleasure is 'a good', not *the* good, as 'any good thing' is made 'more desirable', by adding another to it (p. 256). Plato used this line of argument to disprove 'the view that pleasure is the good', by saying that 'intelligence' makes 'the life of pleasure' more desirable (p. 256). Nothing can be 'the good', if adding something to it makes it 'more desirable'; we need to find something that cannot be 'made better' in this way (p. 256).

iii The view that pleasure is not a good is also open to criticism (pp. 256–9)

It is 'nonsense' to argue that what 'all creatures try to obtain is not a good', especially as 'intelligent', as well as 'irrational creatures', are 'attracted by pleasure' (pp. 256–7). The contention that it does not follow, from pain's being 'an evil', that 'pleasure is a good', is not convincing either (p. 257). If pleasure and pain are both 'evils', they would both be 'objects of aversion', and, if they are both 'neutral', they would both be, or not be, 'equally objects of aversion' (p. 257). In fact, people choose the first 'as a good', and shun the second 'as an evil' (p. 257).

Some say that, whereas good is '**determinate**', pleasure is 'indeterminate', as there are degrees of it; but this applies to 'justice and all the other virtues' (p. 257). Just as people are 'pleased in different degrees', they are also 'more just', 'more brave', and so on (p. 257). Further, there are both '**pure and mixed**' **pleasures** (p. 257). And why should not pleasure be 'determinate' in the way that 'health is', which 'admits of degrees', and is not present, in 'the same proportion', in everyone, or in 'the same person' all the time (p. 258)?

Their assumption is that the good is perfect, that

'movements and processes are incomplete', and that pleasure is 'a movement or process' (p. 258). But this seems wrong. It is said the pleasure is 'replenishment' of 'our natural condition', but this is a *bodily* experience, so what would then 'feel pleasure' is that in which 'the replenishment takes place': 'the body'. But this is 'not generally accepted', and seems to arise from the pleasures of eating: it is thought that, because we experience 'a lack', we 'subsequently find pleasure in replenishment' (p. 258).

Even the view that some pleasures are bad can be challenged (pp. 259–60). Those who say there are 'disreputable pleasures' can be refuted by the argument that some of these are only 'pleasant' to people 'of an unhealthy disposition', while others are not 'desirable', if 'achieved in a certain way', as when wealth is obtained by 'treason' (p. 259). Pleasures also 'differ in kind' (p. 259). Those arising from 'noble acts' are not the same as those arising from 'base ones'; it is impossible, for example, to enjoy 'the pleasure of a just man unless one is just' (p. 259).

Further, no one would elect to have a child's 'mentality', even if this meant deriving 'the greatest pleasure' from 'things that children like', or enjoy a 'disgraceful' activity, even if there were no 'painful consequences'; and we wish to have many things, such as 'memory' and 'knowledge', even if they bring no pleasure (p. 260). Pleasure seems not to be 'the good', as 'not every pleasure is desirable', and some pleasures that are 'desirable in themselves' are superior 'in kind', or due to their 'sources' (p. 260).

iv. Pleasure is not a process (pp. 260–2)

Pleasure, like the 'act of seeing', seems to be 'complete at any moment': there is nothing, prolongation of which will 'enable its specific quality to be perfected'; so it is not 'a process' (p. 260). A 'movement', for example, is not 'complete at any given time': the 'several movements are incomplete, and differ in kind, since the terminal points constitute specific differences' (p. 261). Pleasure, however, 'is complete at any given moment' (p. 261). We can also see that 'a movement must occupy time, whereas a feeling of pleasure does not' (p. 262).

The relation of pleasure to activity (pp. 262–3). The 'activity of any sense is at its best when the organ is in the best condition and directed towards the best of the objects proper to that sense'; and this activity 'will be most perfect and most pleasurable' (p. 262). Each sense has its 'corresponding' pleasure, which 'perfects the activity', and this will occur as long as 'the object of thought or sensation', and that which 'judges or contemplates', are 'in the right condition' (p. 263).

Why does nobody feel 'pleasure continuously' (p. 263)? The reason is 'probably fatigue', as no 'human faculty can be continuously active' (p. 263). Again, things 'please us while they are novelties', but then cease to do so (p. 263).

Pleasure is essential to life (pp. 263–4). All are 'drawn towards pleasure', as they are 'eager to live', directing their activities towards 'those objects', and through 'those faculties', they like best; pleasure 'perfects the activities', and 'so perfects life' (p. 263–4). We need not worry here about whether we 'choose life on account of pleasure', or vice versa: they are 'closely connected', and, just as there is no pleasure 'without activity', every 'activity is perfected by its pleasure' (p. 264).

v As activities differ in kind, so do their pleasures (pp. 264–7)

Pleasures 'differ in kind', as can be seen from the 'close connection of each pleasure with the activity that it perfects'

(p. 264). Pleasures 'intensify their activities'; what intensifies something is 'proper to it'; and things that are 'proper to things that are different' are different themselves (p. 265). Activities are also 'hindered' by pleasures relating to 'other activities' (p. 265). If someone is doing two things, the 'more pleasurable' one 'interferes with the other' (p. 265). 'Alien pleasures' affect people in the same way as 'pain', and are 'destructive' of activities, although 'not to the same degree' (p. 265).

The pleasure 'proper to a serious activity is virtuous', and that to a 'bad one is vicious' (pp. 265–6). Pleasures are 'as diverse as their activities', but 'intellectual pleasures are superior to sensuous ones', and both sorts 'differ among themselves' (p. 266). Every animal is thought to have 'a proper pleasure': that of exercising its 'proper function' (p. 266). Different 'species of animals' have 'different kinds of pleasures', but it would be 'reasonable' to expect those of 'the same species' to be 'uniform' (p. 266). However, with human beings, the 'same things delight one set of people and annoy another', just like 'sweet things', which do not 'taste the same to a feverish patient' as to a 'normal person' (p. 266).

Only the good man's pleasures are real and truly human (p. 267). We accept the 'good man's view' as 'the true one', so 'true pleasures' will be the ones 'he enjoys' (p. 267). Those that 'displease him' (the 'admittedly disreputable' ones) are not 'pleasures at all'; only 'the depraved' will find them pleasant (p. 267). Only investigation of 'human activities' can show whether there is one 'reputable' pleasure that can be regarded as 'the pleasure of man' (p. 267).

Book X

vi Recapitulation: the nature of happiness (pp. 267–9)

Happiness is not 'a *state*': if it were, a man 'who slept all through his life' might possess it (pp. 267–8). It relates to 'some activity', and, as these are either 'chosen for themselves', or for 'the sake of something else', we must 'class happiness' as the former, because it is 'self-sufficient' and needs nothing else (p. 268). Such activities are those 'from which nothing is required beyond the exercise of the activity', and this 'description' fits 'actions that accord with goodness' (p. 268).

Happiness must be distinguished from amusement (pp. 268–9). 'Pleasant amusements' are put in 'this class', because they are not 'means to something else'; but they lead people to 'neglect their bodies' and 'property' (p. 268). However, as many, regarded as happy, including those 'in positions of power', engage in 'such occupations', it is held that they are 'conducive to happiness' (p. 268). But 'virtue and intelligence', the 'sources of serious activities', are not dependent on 'positions of power', and the fact that such people, who may never have experienced '**refined pleasure**', resort to '**physical pleasures**', is no reason for regarding them as a worthy choice (pp. 268–9). Different things seem 'valuable' to 'good and bad men', and it is the things the former think 'valuable' that are 'really such'; and this is 'virtuous activity' (p. 269). It would be 'paradoxical' for us to labour through life, just 'to amuse ourselves' (p. 269).

We choose almost everything, 'except happiness', for 'the sake of something else' (p. 269). The 'happy life' is lived 'in accordance with goodness', suggesting 'seriousness', not 'amusing oneself' (p. 269). The 'activity of a man' is 'always more serious in proportion as it is better', so the 'activity of the better part is superior' and 'more conducive to happiness' (p. 269). Anyone can enjoy 'bodily pleasures', but happiness is

not found in these, but in 'activities in accordance with virtue'
(p. 269).

vii *Happiness and contemplation (pp. 270–3)*

If this is the case, (perfect) happiness is an activity 'in accordance with the highest virtue', whether 'the intellect', or something else we see as 'naturally ruling and guiding us', and
which may be 'divine', or more so than 'any other part of us'
(p. 270). This is 'contemplative activity', for the intellect is
'the highest thing in us'; apprehends 'the highest things that
can be known'; and, unlike any 'practical activity', can be performed continuously (p. 270). Also, happiness must contain
'pleasure', and those who 'possess knowledge pass their time
more pleasantly' than those pursuing it (pp. 270–1). 'Self-
sufficiency' is also a 'quality' of 'contemplative activity': while
the 'just man' (and 'similarly', the 'temperate' and 'brave' one)
needs people towards whom he can be just, and so on, the
'wise man' can 'practise contemplation' alone, and so is 'the
most self-sufficient of men' (p. 270). Contemplation is also
'appreciated for its own sake', as nothing else is expected to be
'gained from it' (p. 271).

Since happiness is thought to imply leisure, it must be an intel-
lectual, not a practical activity (pp. 271–2). It is 'commonly believed' that 'happiness depends on leisure', but the 'practical
virtues' are exercised in 'politics' or 'warfare', which has no
room for it (p. 271). Politics, for example, is securing 'the happiness of the politician himself and of his fellow-citizens': a
happiness that is 'separate from politics' (p. 271). So, if 'politics
and warfare', though 'pre-eminent in nobility and grandeur',
are 'incompatible with leisure', and 'directed towards some
other end', whereas intellectual activity, in the 'form of con-

templation', aims at no 'other end beyond itself', and has 'a
pleasure peculiar to itself', it will be 'the perfect happiness for
man': provided he has 'a full span of life', as nothing pertain-
ing to 'happiness is incomplete' (pp. 271–2).

*Life on this plane is not too high for the divine element in
human nature (pp. 272–3)*. This life is 'too high for human
attainment', and one living it will do so, through 'something
divine within him' (p. 272). To the extent that this 'divine element is superior to the **composite being**', so its activity will 'be
superior to that of the other kind of virtue': if the 'intellect is
divine compared with man', intellectual life must be divine,
compared to that of 'a human being' (p. 272). We must not
heed those who say we should 'think the thoughts of man',
but 'put on immortality', and live in keeping with 'the highest that is in us' (p. 272). Indeed, this seems to be 'the true
self of the individual' (p. 272). What is 'best and most pleasant' for any 'creature' is what is 'proper to it', and, for human
beings, the 'most pleasant life', and therefore 'the happiest', is
that 'of the intellect', as this is 'in the fullest sense the man'
(pp. 272–3).

viii *Moral activity is secondary happiness (pp. 273–4)*

A life conforming to 'the other kind of virtue' will be 'happy
in a secondary degree': it is in our relations with each other
that we 'act justly and bravely', and these are '*human* experiences' (p. 273). 'Moral goodness' is 'intimately connected' with
'the feelings', and it and prudence are 'closely linked', as 'the
moral virtues' provide the 'first principles of prudence', while
prudence sets 'the right standard for the virtues' (p. 273). The
link between the 'moral virtues' and 'the feelings' means
that the former 'belong to the composite person', so living in

conformity with them, and its associated happiness, is 'also human' (p. 273). The 'happiness of the intellect is separate', but 'detailed treatment' of it would go outside 'our present inquiry' (p. 273). It requires fewer 'external accessories' than 'moral goodness' (p. 273). For example, the 'liberal man' needs money to act liberally (p. 274).

Do 'actions' or 'intention' play the bigger part in 'determining the goodness of conduct' (p. 274)? Its 'perfection' would require both, and, unlike 'contemplative' activity, 'many accessories' may be needed to perform 'virtuous actions' (p. 274). However, as a 'human being' and 'member of society', the individual 'chooses to act in accordance with virtue', and needs 'external goods' to do so (p. 274).

The view that happiness is contemplation is confirmed by other arguments (pp. 274–6). There is another argument for happiness being 'a kind of contemplative activity' (p. 274). We think of the gods as 'supremely happy and blessed', but 'what kind of actions' do they perform (p. 274)? If we enumerated 'the whole list' of such actions as being brave, liberal or temperate, we would find that 'the practical details' are 'petty and unworthy of gods' (p. 275). As we consider them to be 'living' and 'active' beings, the only activity left is 'contemplation'; so, 'among human activities', it is the one 'most akin' to that of the gods and 'the happiest' (p. 275). This is confirmed by the 'lower animals' having no 'share in happiness', because they are 'incapable' of contemplation, while human life is happy, to the extent that it 'contains something' resembling 'the divine activity' (p. 275). The 'more people contemplate, the happier they are' as a result of it.

However, as they are human, they also require 'external felicity', in the form of healthy bodies and the availability of food (p. 275). But happiness does not require many of these 'external goods': neither 'self-sufficiency' nor 'moral conduct' require a 'superfluity of means', and 'private persons' are thought to perform more 'decent actions' than those 'in positions of power' (p. 275–6). Solon was right to say that 'happy people' are those 'moderately equipped with external goods', who live 'temperate lives', and achieve 'the finest deeds' (p. 276). **Anaxagoras** did not believe that wealth or power are essential to happiness either, although he thought that this seemed 'an oddity' to most people, who judge 'by outward appearances' (p. 276). But we need to test all this against 'the facts' and 'actual life' (p. 276). One who uses 'his intellect' is likely to have 'the best state of mind', and to be 'loved by the gods', as they 'take pleasure' in the part of human beings that is 'best' and closest to themselves: thus, they 'reward' the 'wise man', and hold him 'dearest', so it is 'natural that he should also be the happiest of men' (p. 276).

ix So much for ethical theory. How can it be put into practice? (pp. 277–84)

Have we done enough by outlining 'happiness and the several virtues', or is the important thing, with conduct, to put 'our knowledge into practice', and 'become good ourselves' (p. 277)? Mere 'discourses' may be able to make a 'truly idealistic character susceptible of virtue', but it will not impel 'the masses towards human perfection', as they are 'ruled by fear', not 'shame'; are deterred 'from evil' by 'punishments', not 'disgrace'; and have no 'conception' of what is 'fine and truly pleasurable' (p. 277). It is impossible for any 'argument' to overcome 'habits long embedded in the character', so we must 'be content' if what is 'supposed to make us good enables us to attain some portion of goodness' (pp. 277–8).

Goodness can only be induced in a suitably receptive character (p. 278). There are different views about how people 'become good': whether it is by 'nature', 'habit' or 'instruction' (p. 278). Nature is 'beyond our control', while 'discussion and instruction' do not always work: they cannot 'dissuade' one who lives by his 'feelings', as these yield 'only to force' (p. 278). We need 'a character to work on' with 'some affinity to virtue', and which 'appreciates what is noble' (p. 278).

Education in goodness is best undertaken by the state (pp. 278–9). 'Right training for goodness' is hard to obtain, except for those raised 'under right laws' (p. 278). Thus, 'upbringing and occupations' must be 'regulated by law', as they will not be 'irksome', once they are 'habitual', and this regulation of 'activities' needs to continue throughout 'the whole of life' (pp. 278–9). People respond to 'compulsion and punishment' more readily than to 'argument', which is why many say that 'legislators' need to 'inflict chastisement' on the disobedient, and 'deport the incorrigible', as well as appealing to the 'finer feelings' of those whose habits have been shaped by 'a decent training': the 'good man' will 'listen to reason', but the 'bad one' has to be 'controlled by pain' (p. 279).

So, if right upbringing, training in 'right habits' and 'reputable occupations' are necessary for producing 'a good man', people require 'guidance' by a 'right system'; and this must be the 'law', which uses 'compulsion', and has the advantage over 'human agents' that its restrictions on the 'impulses' are not resented (p. 279). However, it is only 'in **Sparta**' that 'the lawgiver' is concerned with 'upbringing and daily life'; most states have 'completely neglected' these matters' (p. 279).

If neglected by the state, it can be supplied by the parent; but it calls for some knowledge of legislative science (pp. 280–1). If the state does not do this, the individual must take on 'the role of

Book X

legislator', and help his children towards 'goodness'; a father's 'instructions and habits' carry the same weight, 'in the household', as laws do in the state (p. 280). They have the advantage over 'the public sort' of being influenced by 'natural affection', and, because 'individual attention is given', of being 'more accurate', as 'each person' receives 'what suits him': a 'boxing instructor', for example, does not 'make all his pupils adopt the same manner of fighting' (p. 280). However, the 'best detailed treatment' will be given by the 'instructor' with 'general knowledge of what is good for all cases, or for a specific type'; 'the sciences' concern 'common facts', so one who wishes to be 'professionally qualified with theoretical knowledge' must study 'the universal' (pp. 280–1). Thus, if we take it that people can 'be made good by laws', someone who wishes to 'make other people' better should 'acquire the art of legislation' (p. 281). If anyone can produce a 'right disposition' in someone else, it is the 'man with knowledge' (p. 281).

Where can such knowledge be obtained? Not from the sophists (pp. 281–3). How can we learn about 'legislation' (p. 281)? The obvious answer, as it is a 'branch of political science', is 'from the politicians' (p. 281). But the situation is not like that in other 'sciences and faculties', such as medicine, where the same people are both practitioners and teachers (p. 281). The '**sophists** profess to teach' political science, but it is the politicians who practise it, on the basis of 'experience', rather than 'the exercise of reason' (p. 281). And, although the politicians could leave no 'finer legacy to their countries' than to write or lecture 'about political subjects', it does seem that experience is a major contributor to 'success in politics' (p. 281–2).

The sophists are 'ignorant' of the subject, equating it with 'rhetoric', and believing it is easy to 'frame a constitution', by selecting from the 'most highly approved' laws: as if this did not demand 'understanding' and 'correct judgement', which only 'the experts' possess (p. 282). Laws are 'the products of the art of politics': they cannot teach people 'the art of legislation' (p. 282). 'Reading handbooks' cannot equip someone to practise medicine, as it will only be 'helpful to the experienced' (p. 282). Similarly, 'collections of laws' will only 'be serviceable' to those with a 'formed habit of mind', who are able to judge 'what is rightly enacted' (p. 283).

The student of ethics must therefore apply himself to politics (pp. 283–4). Thus, we should investigate the questions of 'legislation' and 'constitutions generally' 'more closely', to make our 'philosophy of human conduct' as 'complete as possible' (p. 283). We need to review any 'valid statements' that have been made previously; decide, by looking at constitutions, which influences are 'conservative' or 'destructive of a state'; and discover why 'some states are well governed', and others not (pp. 283–4). This may enable us to determine the kind of constitution that 'is the best' and 'the best system of laws and customs' (p. 284).

Overview

The following section is a chapter-by-chapter overview of the five books of Aristotle's *The Nicomachean Ethics*, summarized in this *Briefly*. It is designed for quick reference to the detailed summary above. Readers may also find it particularly helpful for revision.

Book I

The Object of Life (pp. 3–30)

i Every rational activity aims at some end or good. One end (like one activity) may be subordinate to another (pp. 3–4)

Every art and action aims at some good, so the good is what all things aim at. Ends differ, as some are activities, while others are results distinct from the activities. Where ends are distinct from actions, the results are superior to the activities. There are many actions, arts and sciences, so there are many ends. However, many arts come under a single faculty (making bridles, for example, comes under horsemanship, which comes under military science), and the ends of the latter are more important, as the former are pursued for their sake. If activities have an end, desired for its own sake, this must be the good, the supreme good, and it will help us greatly in how to conduct our lives, as we are more likely to achieve our aim with a target.

ii The science that studies the supreme good for man is politics (pp. 4–5)

Politics seems to be the most authoritative science, as things like war and property management come under it, and it determines the subjects taught in states. As it lays down what we should, and should not, do, this end must be the good for man. Even if the good of individual and community coincide, that of the latter seems finer. So, the aim of our investigation is a kind of political science.

iii *Politics is not an exact science (pp. 5–6)*

The account of this will be adequate, if it is as clear as the subject-matter allows. Instances of morally fine and just conduct, which are the concern of political science, vary greatly, and may be thought to be so by convention, not nature. Goods also vary, and can be hurtful, as when people's courage destroys them. A broad outline of the truth must suffice. The educated mind does not look for more precision in a subject than its nature permits.

The student should have some general knowledge and experience of life (p. 6). Everyone judges rightly what he understands, so one with a general education is a good general critic. Lacking experience of the practical business of life, a young man is unfit to study political science. He follows his feelings, and will not benefit from it, as the object is action, not knowledge. But it will be a great help to those, whose actions are based on a principle of knowledge.

iv *The end is no doubt happiness, but views of happiness differ (pp. 6–8)*

Ordinary and cultured people agree that happiness is the highest practical good, and identify it with living well, but they differ as to what it is. The former think it is something like pleasure or money, while a person may change his opinion, saying it is health, when he is ill, and money, when he is hard up. Some have held that, above particular goods, there is something good in itself, which causes goodness in all the others.

Learners must start from beliefs that are accepted or at least familiar (pp. 7–8). Plato rightly pointed out the difference between arguments from and to first principles. Things are known in two ways: to us and absolutely; and we must begin with the former. A serious student of ethics and political science needs training in good habits, for fact is the starting-point. If this is sufficiently clear, there will be no need to find the reason why.

v The three types of life. Neither pleasure nor public honour seems to be an adequate end; the contemplative life will be considered later (pp. 8–9)

The masses believe good or happiness is pleasure. The three main types of life are the one referred to, the political and the contemplative. The masses prefer to live a bovine existence, as do many in positions of power. Cultured people identify the good with honour, the goal of political life. But this is a superficial answer: honour depends on the giver, not the receiver, whereas the good is something proper to its possessor. Also, men seek to be honoured for their goodness, regarding it as superior, so perhaps this is the end pursued in public life. But possessing goodness seems compatible with being asleep, or an inactive life. The contemplative life is considered below. Wealth is only a means to something else, and is not the good we seek. The other suggestions, being appreciated for themselves, are more likely, but are nonetheless inadequate.

*vi   There cannot be a universal good such as Plato held to be
the culmination of his theory of forms (pp. 10–13)*

The universal needs to be examined, although the forms
make this more difficult. This theory's proponents did not put
forward ideas of classes, in which they recognized degrees of
priority.

However, things are called 'good' in the categories of substance, quality and relation, and, as what exists in its own
right, substance, is by nature prior to the relative, there cannot be any common idea in these cases. Also, as things are
called 'good' in as many senses as they are said to exist (as
in the various categories), there cannot be a single universal
common to all cases. It would also mean there would be one
science of all good things, but there are more than one, even
in things coming under one category. Again, it is difficult to
see what is meant by a thing-itself. If the definition of 'man'
is the same in man and man-himself, the good and the good-
itself will not differ as good, while good will not be made any
more so by being eternal. Further, only things good in themselves, which are pursued or esteemed in their own right, are
called good in virtue of one form; those that are just a means
to good are called so in a different sense. The two need to
be distinguished, to determine whether they are called good
in virtue of one idea. Many things, like sight, pleasures and
honours, are regarded as good in themselves, but the question arises as to whether they are or whether nothing is good
in itself, except the idea. But, if this is so, the class is purposeless. Further, if they are good in themselves, the definition of good would have to be the same for all, but as they all
have different definitions in respect of goodness, good is not
a common characteristic corresponding to one idea. Perhaps,
all goods derive from or contribute to one good, or are good

by analogy, but even if the goodness that is predicated in common is one, separately existing thing, it cannot be acquired by human beings. Maybe, we should get to know the goods that can be acquired, which are good for us, but this clashes with the way the practical sciences work: they aim at a good, but not knowledge of it. It would not benefit a joiner to know this good-itself.

vii What is the good for man? It must be the ultimate end or object of human life: something that is in itself completely satisfying. Happiness fits this description (pp. 13–17)

The good we are seeking seems to vary with the action or art, the good of each (it is health in medicine, for example) being the end for which everything else is done; and if one thing is the end of all actions, it is the practical good. However, some of our chosen ends, like wealth, are means to something else, and, unlike the supreme good, not final ends. An end that can never be chosen for the sake of another is more final than those that can. The end that is chosen only for its own sake is final without qualification. Happiness, which is chosen for itself, and never for anything else's sake, is regarded as such an end, whereas things like honour are chosen for themselves, but also for its sake. Again, the perfect good is one that, by itself, makes life desirable, and happiness does. Addition of another good does not make it more desirable: it is the end to which our actions are directed.

But what is happiness? If we consider what the function of man is, we find that happiness is a virtuous activity of the soul (pp. 15–16). We can define happiness by grasping the function of man. The goodness of any group of people (like sculptors), who perform a specific activity, is its performance. Just as the limbs have a function, human beings do, over and above particular ones. Man's proper function is not nutrition and growth, or sentient life, which he shares with plants and animals, but an activity of the soul, in accordance with a rational principle. Now, the function of an individual, and a good individual of the same kind, is generically the same: a harpist's function is to play the harp, that of a good one to play it well. If a man's function is as stated above, that of a good man is to lead this kind of life well. The good for man is an activity of the soul in accordance with (the best kind of) virtue, and this must take place over a complete lifetime.

This sketch can be elaborated later, but great precision is not to be expected (pp. 16–17). This is only an outline account of the good. We must look for only the degree of precision the subject-matter permits, and not allow side issues to swamp the main ones.

viii Our view of happiness is supported by popular beliefs (pp. 18–20)

This principle must be examined in the light of what is commonly said about it. Our definition is supported by the fact that goods have been put into three classes: external, of the soul and of the body, of which the second are good in the fullest sense. It is also right to say that the end consists in certain actions, putting it among the goods of the soul. Our definition is also supported by the belief that the happy man lives well, as we have described it as a kind of good life. It also includes all the required constituents of happiness, which some believe to be virtue, others prudence, and so on. An important point is whether the supreme good is to possess or exercise virtue, for the former, unlike the latter, could be present in someone, but produce no good result. Virtuous actions are pleasant in themselves, and give the lover of virtue pleasure, so nothing needs to be added to his life. One who does not delight in fine actions is not good, for such actions are good and fine in the highest degree. Thus, happiness is the best, finest and most pleasurable thing of all, but it needs external goods, as it is hard to do fine deeds without resources, while people are not happy if, for example, they are solitary, suggesting that it requires some prosperity.

ix How is happiness acquired? (pp. 20–2)

Happiness would be a suitable gift from the gods, but if it is acquired through moral goodness and training, this would mean it is widely shared, as it is attainable by anyone, not incapable of goodness. This view fits in with the definition of happiness as a kind of virtuous activity of the soul, whereas other goods serve as its instruments. We have said that political science's end is the highest good, and its main concern is to make citizens virtuous and ready to do fine deeds. Animals, who are incapable of it, and children, who are too young (happiness requires a complete life), cannot be happy.

x Is it only when his life is completed that a man can rightly be called happy? (pp. 22–5)

Perhaps, no one is happy while alive, but, having defined happiness as a kind of activity, it seems paradoxical to say people are really happy, when dead. It is difficult to deny that the dead are happy, given the popular belief that good or evil touches them, and the absurdity of maintaining that they are unaffected by what befalls their descendants. But, if someone is called happy, not because he is, but was, it would be equally absurd to deny that it can be truly stated of him when he is. Changes of fortune are immaterial, because success and failure in life do not depend on them: it is virtuous activities that determine our happiness. The happy man will be happy throughout life, as he will spend most of it in virtuous conduct and contemplation.

He cannot become miserable, for he will never do hateful and mean things, and ordinary misfortunes will not disrupt his happiness. He is active in accordance with complete virtue, and has enough external goods through a complete life and when he dies, for happiness is an utterly final and complete end. Thus, the living, who have these qualifications, are supremely happy, but with a human happiness.

xi Are the dead affected by the fortunes of those who survive them? (pp. 25–6)

Thinking the dead are unaffected by their descendants' fortunes is against accepted beliefs. Someone's misfortunes, or those of his friends, may influence his life powerfully or trivially, so it is debatable whether or not the dead participate in the good or its opposite. They are probably affected to some extent by loved ones' fortunes but the effect will be slight.

xii Is happiness to be praised as a means or valued as an end? (pp. 26–7)

Should we praise or value happiness? Things are praised, when related to something else, as virtue is praised for the effects it produces. If praise belongs to the relative, the best things demand something greater and better, as when the gods are called 'blessed'. Eudoxus said that pleasure's not being praised shows its superiority to other goods. Happiness is a first principle: we do everything else for its sake, and hold that the first principle and cause of what is good is precious and divine.

xiii To understand what moral goodness is we must study the soul of man (pp. 27–30)

Examining the nature of virtue will enable us to form a view about happiness. The true statesman studies the former thoroughly, as he wants his fellow-citizens to be good and law-abiding. Our concern is with human goodness, the goodness of the soul, for we are interested in the good or happiness for man. The statesman needs to study the soul, but with a view to politics and sufficiently for that purpose.

The several faculties of the soul distinguished (pp. 28–30). The findings of psychology can be used. The soul is partly rational and partly irrational, and the vegetative part of the latter has no part in human goodness. There is another irrational element in the soul, which fights against the rational, as in the urges of those lacking self-control. But it seems to be amenable to reason: in self-controlled people, it obeys reason, and is in harmony with it in the brave and temperate. So, the appetitive part of the soul responds to reason by obeying it. On the other hand, if the appetitive part is classed as rational, there are two rational parts, with the relation of the appetitive to the rational part proper being that of a child heeding its father. There are two corresponding classes of virtue: intellectual, like wisdom, understanding and prudence, which are referred to when someone is praised for his state of mind; and moral, like liberality and temperance, which relate to character.

Book II

Moral Goodness (pp. 31–49)

i Moral virtues, like crafts, are acquired by practice and habituation (pp. 31–2)

Either virtue is intellectual, resulting from instruction, or moral, resulting from habit. Human beings are constituted to receive the moral virtues, but their full development is due to habit. As with the arts, we acquire the virtues by exercising them. People become just by performing just acts, and every legislator's aim is to make his citizens good by habituation. The means of bringing about any form of excellence are the same as those that destroy it. People become good or bad builders by building well or badly, and the same is true of the virtues. The sort of habits we form from the earliest age matter a lot.

ii In practical sciences so much depends upon particular circumstances that only general rules can be given (pp. 33–5)

As we are studying how to become good men, not what goodness is, we must think about how to perform our actions, as these determine our dispositions: we should act according to the right principle. It is as difficult to lay down hard and fast rules about conduct as about what is healthy, and, if this is true of the general rule, it is even more so with its application to particular problems. We have to think about what the circumstances demand.

A cardinal rule: right conduct is incompatible with excess or deficiency in feelings and actions (p. 34). However, just as eating and drinking too much or too little destroys health, moral qualities are destroyed by deficiency or excess. One who fears everything and stands up to nothing turns into a coward, while one who fears nothing at all becomes foolhardy. Temperance and courage are destroyed by excess and deficiency, and preserved by the mean.

Our virtues are exercised in the same kinds of action as gave rise to them (pp. 34–5). Just as the same sort of actions promote and destroy the virtues, the activities that flow from them will also be the same sort of actions. We become temperate by refraining from pleasures, and can best refrain from pleasures when we are temperate.

iii The pleasure or pain that actions cause the agent may serve as an index of moral progress, since good conduct consists in a proper attitude towards pleasure and pain (pp. 35–7)

The pleasure or pain accompanying people's acts indicates their dispositions. One facing danger gladly is brave, whereas one feeling distress is a coward. Moral goodness is about pleasures and pains: the first make us behave badly, the second deter us from fine actions. Plato pointed out the importance of being educated to feel joy and grief at the right things. Punishment uses pleasures and pains, and people become bad through them, by seeking, or shunning, the wrong ones. Three factors, the fine, advantageous and pleasant, lead to choice; three, the base, harmful and painful, to avoidance. The good man goes right with these and the bad one does not. We also regulate our actions by pleasure and pain, and they greatly influence our conduct. Heraclitus says it is hard to fight against pleasure, so morality and political science must address the issue of pleasures and pains, as those treating them rightly will be good, while those treating them wrongly will be bad.

iv Acts that are incidentally virtuous distinguished from those that are done knowingly, of choice and from a virtuous disposition (pp. 37–8)

It is hard to understand how people must perform just actions to become just: if they act justly, they are so already. But virtuous acts are not done in a just way, merely by having a certain quality, but only if the agent knows what he is doing; chooses it for its own sake; and does so from a permanent disposition. Someone is just or temperate, not merely by doing such acts, but by doing them as just and temperate men do. So, people do become just by performing just acts; and nobody can become good by not doing them. But most people do not do so: they rely on theory, and think they are being philosophical.

v In order to define virtue we must decide to what class or genus it belongs. It is not a feeling or a faculty, but a disposition (pp. 38–9)

Virtue must be one of the three kinds of modification, feelings, faculties and dispositions, found in the soul. By the first, is meant desire, anger, fear, and so on; by the second, our being able to have such feelings; by the third, the conditions of being well- or ill-disposed towards them. Thus, our disposition towards anger is good, if we have a moderate tendency towards it. Virtues and vices are not feelings; we are not called good or bad on account of our feelings. Virtues, unlike feelings, are expressions of choice, and they are not faculties either. We are not praised or blamed for being capable of feeling. Nature gives us faculties, but does not make us good or bad. Virtues are dispositions.

Overview

vi But what is its differentia? Any excellence enables its possessor to function well; therefore this is true of human excellence, i.e. virtue (pp. 39–41)

As to the kind of disposition, any kind of excellence makes that of which it is the excellence good, and makes it perform its function well. Human excellence is the disposition that makes someone a good man and causes him to perform his function well.

This is confirmed by the doctrine of the mean (pp. 40–1). With something that is continuous and divisible, there can be a part that is greater than, less than, or equal to, the rest. The third of these is a mean between excess and deficiency, and it is the same for everybody. There is also a mean in relation to us. Ten pounds is a lot of food, and two pounds a little, but a trainer would not necessarily prescribe six for a particular athlete, as it might be too much or too little for him. Knowledgeable people seek the second mean, which is relative to them, and this is the mean that moral virtue, which concerns feelings and actions, aims to hit. It is possible, and wrong, to feel fear, anger, pleasure, and so on, too much or too little. The right way is to have them to an intermediate degree; and the same applies to actions. Excess and deficiency are failings, but the mean is a success, although it is a difficult target to hit.

A provisional definition of virtue (p. 42). Virtue, then, is a purposive disposition. It lies in a mean between the vices of excess and deficiency; is relative to us; and is determined by a rational principle. In essence, it is a mean, but in respect of what is right and best, it is an extreme.

But the rule of choosing the mean cannot be applied to some actions and feelings, which are essentially evil (pp. 42–3). There is no mean in relation to such feelings and actions as malice and murder, which are not evil through excess or deficiency, but are evil in themselves. Just as there is no mean, excess or deficiency in courage, as the mean here is an extreme, the same is true of these vices. Excess and deficiency do not admit of a mean, nor does a mean admit of excess and deficiency.

vii The doctrine of the mean applied to particular virtues (pp. 43–6)

All this must be applied to particular cases. With fear and confidence, courage is the mean, and those whose confidence is excessive or deficient are rash or cowardly. With giving money, liberality is the mean and prodigality and illiberality the excess and deficiency. One whose aspirations go too far is ambitious, one falling short in them unambitious, but the mean has no name. Here, the intermediate man may sometimes be regarded as ambitious or unambitious. In relation to anger, the mean is patience, and the extremes irascibility and lack of spirit. Means exist in social intercourse. With truth, truthfulness is the mean, boastfulness and irony the extremes. Pleasantness in social entertainment is wit, the excess buffoonery and the deficiency boorishness. In life generally, friendliness is the mean, and the extremes flattery and ill-temperedness. There are mean states in the sphere of feelings. Righteous indignation, for example, is the mean between envy and spite, which concern feelings of pleasure or pain at the experiences of our neighbours.

viii The mean is often nearer to one extreme than to the other, or seems nearer because of our natural tendencies (pp. 46–7)

The extremes of excess and deficiency are contrary to the mean and to each other, and the mean to the extremes. The mean states are excessive, compared with the deficient, and deficient compared with the excessive. A brave man seems rash compared with a coward, and cowardly compared with a rash man, but the greatest contrast is between the two extremes. But either deficiency or excess may be more opposed to the mean: the direct opposite of courage is cowardice, not rashness. We tend to oppose to the mean the extreme that is further from it, and also to view the things we are more inclined towards as more opposed to the mean. As we are inclined towards pleasures, we regard licentiousness as being contrary to temperance.

ix Summing-up of the foregoing discussion, together with three practical rules for good conduct (pp. 48–9)

Moral virtue is a mean, aiming at the mean point in feelings and actions, which is difficult to do: it is easy to get angry, but not to feel or act towards the right person, to the right extent, at the right time, for the right reason and in the right way. We need to avoid the extreme that is more contrary to the mean, and choose the lesser of two evils; be aware of our own common errors, and force ourselves in the opposite direction; and be vigilant about pleasure and pleasant things, as we do not judge them impartially. Following these rules is the best way to hit the mean. There seems to be no right way to be angry, so we sometimes praise deficiency as patience, and temper as manliness. Small deviations from the right degree are not usually censured, but it is hard to say how long, and how much, a man may go wrong before being blamed.

Book III

Moral Responsibility: Two Virtues (pp. 50–81)

i *Actions are voluntary, involuntary or non-voluntary*
(pp. 50–4)

Voluntary actions are praised or blamed, involuntary ones pardoned, so students of moral goodness must determine the limits of the voluntary and involuntary. The latter result from compulsion (they have an external origin), or ignorance. But the dividing-line is not clear-cut. A tyrant might force someone into dishonourable actions, on threat of harming his parents or children. Such actions are mixed. The agent acts voluntarily, in that he has the power either to do or not do them, but would not choose to do this kind of thing in itself.

There are also some things which people would rather die than do, and agents are praised or blamed, depending on whether or not they have yielded to compulsion. Strictly, compulsory acts are those where the cause is external and the agent contributes nothing. Acts originating in the agent, though involuntary in themselves, are voluntary at the given time and cost. Treating pleasurable and admirable things as having a compulsive effect would make all acts compulsory, as every act is done for their sake. The agent cannot blame external factors, when he succumbs easily to them, and attributes fine acts to himself, but disgraceful ones to pleasure. An act, done through ignorance, is non-voluntary, provided the agent feels pain and repentance.

It is not ignorance in the choice, or of the moral principle, which makes an act involuntary, but ignorance of the particular circumstances. These relate to the agent (although he cannot be ignorant of himself); the act (he may not realize what he is doing); the object of the act (he may be mistaken about his enemy); the instrument (as when he thinks a sharp-pointed spear has a button on it); the aim (as when the agent kills someone with what was intended as a life-saving drug); the manner (he might hit someone, when only meaning to seize his hand). Anyone, ignorant of such particular circumstances, is deemed to have acted involuntarily, but must feel distress.

Voluntary acts originate in the agent, who is aware of all the circumstances. We must not claim that only our discreditable actions are done involuntarily. It is also wrong to call acts, to which we are rightly attracted, involuntary. Some things should make us angry, while we should desire others, such as health and learning. There is no distinction, in terms of voluntariness, between wrong actions that are deliberate and those due to temper, as both irrational feelings and considered judgements are part of human nature. Both must be avoided.

ii Moral conduct implies choice, but what is choice? It must be distinguished from desire, temper, wish and opinion (pp. 54–6)

Choice and moral goodness are closely related. It is wrong to identify choice with desire, which can be contrary to choice, while desire, but not choice, concerns the pleasurable and painful. One can wish for, but not choose, the impossible, such as immortality, and for results that one cannot bring about oneself. Wishing is concerned with the end, choice with the means: we say we wish to be happy, but not that we choose to be. As for opinions, they are true or false, not good or bad like choices, which concern choosing the right object, rather than being correct. Moral defect prevents some, who are good at forming opinions, from making the right choices. The specific quality of choice is being the result of previous deliberation, for it implies a rational principle and thought.

iii If choice involves deliberation, what is the sphere of the latter? (pp. 57–9)

We do not deliberate about such things as eternal facts (for example, the order of the universe), or regular processes, like the rising of the sun. Deliberation concerns practical measures that lie in our power, and which concern us. We deliberate about effects, produced by our agency, as in medicine and finance. Generally, we deliberate about things where the right course is not clear, so the arts, about which we are less certain, call for more deliberation than the sciences.

Deliberation is about means, not ends (pp. 58–9). Deliberation is about means. A statesman does not deliberate about whether to produce law and order, nor a doctor about whether to cure his patient. They set the end, and then consider the means of attaining it. As long as the end is attainable (by our agency), they set about doing it. Man is the originating cause of actions, and deliberation relates to what is practicable for the agent, whose object is the means to ends. Deliberation and choice have the same objects, but the latter has already been determined, as the result of the former.

Definition of choice (p. 59). Choice is a deliberate appetition for things that are in our power. After deciding, through deliberation, we direct our aim.

iv The object of wish is in one sense the good, in another the apparent good (p. 60)

Wishing concerns an end. Some think its object is the good, others the apparent good. The first group think a person choosing wrongly means that what he wishes is not an object of wishing, because, to be wishable, it must be good; the second group that nothing is wishable by nature, but that what the individual considers good is wishable for him. Perhaps, we should say that the object of our wish is the good, but, to the individual, it is what seems good. With a good man, this will be the true good, but, with a bad one, it could be anything. The former judges every situation rightly, and is a standard of what is fine and pleasant. Pleasure deceives many; it appears good to them, and they choose it as good, shunning pain as evil.

v Actions that we initiate ourselves, whether they are good or bad, are voluntary (p. 61)

The end is an object of wishing, and the means objects of deliberation and choice, so actions relating to the latter are done voluntarily. The exercise of the moral virtues relates to the means, so both virtue and vice are in our power. We can do what is right, and not do what is wrong. This is the essence of being good or bad: we decide whether to be decent or worthless. Clearly, if we are the initiators of our own actions, they originate in us, and are in our power.

This is borne out by the common use of rewards and punishments (p. 62). Use of rewards for fine actions, and punishments for wrongdoers, supports this view, as they are designed to encourage the former and restrain the latter.

Responsibility for the results of bad moral states (p. 62). People are punished for ignorance, if responsible for it. A drunkard who commits a crime was capable of not getting drunk, while ignorance of points of law, which should be known, is punished. People live irresponsibly, and their moral state is the result of their way of life. They develop qualities that correspond to their activities, making themselves unjust or licentious, through dishonesty or drinking.

A bad moral state, once formed, is not easily amended (p. 63). It is unreasonable to think that one who acts unjustly or licentiously does not do so voluntarily, but this does not mean he can stop, if he wants to. Unjust and licentious persons have it in their power not to become so, in the first place, but it is then no longer open to them not to be.

Even physical defects, if voluntarily incurred, are culpable (pp. 63–4). Physical defects can be incurred voluntarily, as when people do not take exercise. We pity a person, blind by nature, but condemn one who is blind through heavy drinking. Similarly, with moral defects, we are blamed for the ones we are responsible for.

It may be objected that moral discernment is a gift of nature and cannot be acquired otherwise (p. 64). It can be argued that everybody aims at what appears to be good, but does not control this aim, as it depends on his character: that, if he is not responsible for his moral state, he is not responsible for his view of what is good, or for what he does wrong. One, whose natural disposition is good (they say), has the advantage of what cannot be learned from anybody else: an inborn ability to judge correctly and choose what is truly good.

Even so, virtue will be no more voluntary than vice (p. 65). This would make virtue no more voluntary than vice. But, whether a person's view of the end depends at least partly on himself, or comes from nature, virtue is voluntary, because the good man performs all the means towards the end voluntarily. Vice is no less voluntary, because good and bad men have equal freedom in their actions, even if not in their choice of an end. So, virtues are mean states and dispositions, which are voluntary; enable their possessor to perform the same sort of actions as those by which they were acquired; and to act as the right principle prescribes. However, our actions and dispositions are not voluntary in the same sense. We control the former from beginning to end, the latter only at the beginning.

Now to discuss the virtues one by one (p. 66). Each will be discussed in turn.

vi Courage: the right attitude towards feelings of fear and confidence. What we ought and ought not to fear (pp. 66–7)

Courage is a mean state in relation to feelings of fear and confidence. All evils, such as poverty, sickness and death, are feared, but they do not all concern the courageous man, as the upright man should fear some, like disgrace. One should probably not fear anything, such as poverty or disease, which is not the result of vice or one's own fault, and one is not cowardly for dreading brutality towards his wife and children. Death is the most fearful thing, but not all types offer scope for courage. The noblest form is in war, where the danger is greatest and most glorious, and the courageous man is fearless in the face of honourable or sudden death.

vii Degrees of fear and fearfulness (pp. 67–8)

We do not all find the same things terrible. Some things are said to be beyond human endurance, but differ in the amount of fear they inspire. As far as humanly possible, the courageous man is undaunted, fearing what man naturally fears, but facing it in the right way, and for the sake of what is right and honourable, as this the end of virtue. The wrong thing can be feared, but the courageous man fears the right ones, for the right reason. His courage is noble; he faces dangers for the right motive, performing actions appropriate to his courage.

Excessive fearlessness, rashness and cowardice (pp. 68–9).
One who fears nothing is a maniac or lacks sense. The rash
man wishes to seem as the courageous one really is in his attitude towards fearful situations. The excessively fearful one
is a coward, fearing the wrong things in the wrong way. In
contrast to the courageous man, who is confident, he is also
despondent. The rash man and the coward show excess and
deficiency, but the courageous man, having the right disposition, observes the mean. Courage is a mean state in relation
to confidence and fear, and the courageous man faces danger
as a fine thing to do. Killing oneself is cowardly, as it involves
running away from hardships.

viii Five dispositions that resemble courage (pp. 70–3)

(1) Civic courage (pp. 70–1). This is very like courage. Its ground
is a moral virtue: citizens desire something noble, and wish
to avoid reproach. Those ordered to face death by their commanders are inferior, doing so through fear, not shame: one
should be brave because it is a fine thing.

(2) Experience of risk (pp. 71–2). Experiencing risk, as soldiers do in war, is a form of courage. Of course, experienced
soldiers can make themselves look brave. The best fighters
may not be the bravest, but the strongest and fittest. In extreme
danger, it may be the professional soldiers who flee, while the
citizen troops die at their posts. Unlike the courageous man,
the former fear death more than dishonour.

(3) Spirit or mettle (p. 72). Spirit is also regarded as courage, as it is bold in the face of danger. But, while courageous
people act for a fine motive, animals are not courageous,
just because pain and anger impel them to rush into danger. Quasi-courage, due to spirit, is regarded as courage, if it

includes deliberate choice, but those who fight from pain and anger are not acting from a fine motive, but from feeling.

(4) Sanguineness or optimism (p. 73). Sanguine people are confident, but not courageous: they just regard themselves as the best soldiers, and they run away when things do not turn out as expected. But the courageous man faces up to terrible things, as doing so is a fine act. It is better proof of courage to be undismayed in the face of unexpected, rather than foreseen, alarms: no preparation is involved, so it arises more directly from a person's moral state.

(5) Ignorance (p. 73). Those acting in ignorance only seem courageous. If they discover that things are not as they supposed, they run away.

ix Courage in relation to pleasure and pain (pp. 74–5)

Courage concerns grounds for confidence and fear, but the latter more, as this implies the presence of pain, and should be praised, as it is harder to bear pain than abstain from pleasure. The end of an act involving courage may be pleasant, but the circumstances obscure this. The courageous man bears death and wounds, as a fine thing to do. Death is very distressing to the virtuous man, because his life is so much worth living; but this may make him even braver. Professional soldiers may be less brave, but, having only their lives to lose, are prepared to sell them for petty gains.

x Temperance or self-control, and the pleasures with which it is concerned (pp. 75–6)

Temperance, a mean state with regard to pleasures, is a virtue thought to belong to the irrational parts of the soul.

Pleasures are either psychical or physical (pp. 75–6). There are pleasures of the soul, like love of civic distinction and learning, and bodily ones. Temperance concerns the latter, but not those relating to sight or hearing. With those who enjoy smells, the licentious ones are those who do so by association, as when people enjoy the smell of savoury dishes, which remind them of the objects of their desires.

The grossest pleasures are those of taste and, above all, touch (p. 77). Temperance and licentiousness concern the low, animal pleasures of touch and taste. For the licentious person, it is not the flavours that gratify him, but enjoyment. This, whether in food and drink or sex, depends entirely upon touch. This sense relates to us as animals, not human beings, and to find the greatest satisfaction in it is brutish.

xi Desires or appetites; self-indulgence and insensibility (pp. 77–9)

Desires are either general or particular. Desire for food is natural, as everyone needs it, but, as not everyone desires a particular kind of food, appetite, though it has a natural element, seems a matter of personal taste. The natural desire is just for replenishment of the deficiency, and few go wrong here, except in the direction of too much. With particular pleasures, people err in enjoying the wrong objects, or enjoying things with abnormal intensity, while the licentious show every form of excess. Unlike courage, a man is not called temperate for enduring pain, and licentious for not doing so. The latter desires all pleasant things, before anything else, and, absurdly, feels pain, both when failing to get them and when desiring them. Desiring pleasures less than one ought (deficiency) rarely occurs: such a person would be far from human.

The temperate man does not enjoy wrong pleasures, and is not distressed by the absence of pleasures. He holds a mean position, moderately pursuing pleasures, conducive to health, and which are not dishonourable, or beyond his means; he appreciates them as the right principle directs.

xii Licentiousness is more voluntary than cowardice
(pp. 79–80)

Licentiousness is more voluntary than cowardice, because pain (which the coward tries to avoid), unlike pleasure (which the licentious person chooses), distracts the sufferer. Particular instances of cowardice are seen as unavoidable, as pain can so distract a person that he throws away his weapons and disgraces himself. Though no one desires to be licentious, the licentious man acts as he does from desire and appetite.

Licentious people are like spoilt children (pp. 80–1). Appropriately, children's faults are also called 'licentiousness'. Just as children are impelled by their desires, the appetite for what gives pleasure is insatiable in an irrational being, and exercising it intensifies it, driving out reason. A child must submit to his tutor's directions, and, similarly, the rational principle must control our appetitive element. This needs to be in harmony with the former, with both having as their object attainment of what is admirable. The temperate man desires the right things in the right way at the right time.

Book VI

Intellectual Virtues (pp. 144–66)

i What is the right principle that should regulate conduct? (pp. 144–5)

The mean is what the right principle dictates. In all the above states, there is a target, at which one with this principle aims. There is also a limit that determines the mean states between excess and deficiency, but just saying one should work to a mean is not explicit. We need to know what the right principle is.

Contemplative and calculative intellect (p. 145). We classified some virtues of the soul as of character, others of intellect. We shall now look at the former. The soul has a rational and an irrational part. This also applies to the rational part, which has a part (the scientific) to contemplate things with invariable first principles, and another (the calculative) for variable ones, which differ in kind. We need to understand the best state of both, which will be the state of each.

ii Both kinds of intellect aim at truth, but the calculative faculty aims at truth as rightly desired by the exercise of choice (pp. 146–7)

A thing's virtue relates to its proper function. In the soul, sensation, intellect and appetition control action and attainment of truth. Since moral virtue involves choice, which is deliberate appetition, good choice requires the reasoning to be true and the desire right. This is the practical sense of intellect and truth: the practical intellect's function is to reach the truth that corresponds to right appetition. Choice, originating in appetition, is the efficient cause of action, and involves a certain moral state, for good conduct necessarily involves character as well as thought, as things are only set going by practical thought. Thus, choice is either appetitive intellect or intellectual appetition. Attaining truth is the task of both of the intellectual parts of the soul, and their respective virtues are the states that will best enable them to arrive at it.

iii Five modes of thought or states of mind by which truth is reached (pp. 147–8)

The soul arrives at truth by affirmation or denial in five ways: art, science, prudence, wisdom and intuition. Judgement and opinion are liable to error, and are left out.

Science or scientific knowledge (p. 148). Our assumption is that what is known cannot be otherwise than it is, so necessity is the object of scientific knowledge. It is eternal, cannot come into being or cease to be, and is teachable. It begins from what is already known, as it proceeds either by induction or deduction. It is demonstrative: someone has scientific knowledge when he knows the first principles, and if he does not know them better than the conclusion he draws from them, he will have knowledge only incidentally.

iv Art or technical skill (p. 149)

Variables comprise both products and acts, but these differ. Art is a productive state that is truly reasoned, concerned with bringing something into being, the cause of which is the producer. As production and action are not the same, art must be concerned with the former.

v *Prudence or practical wisdom (pp. 150–1)*

This can be understood by considering the kind of people we
call prudent, who are able to deliberate rightly about what is
conducive to the good life generally: a prudent man is capable
of deliberation. But, as scientific knowledge implies the ability
to demonstrate; as variable things cannot be demonstrated;
and as it is impossible to deliberate about things that are so
necessarily, prudence, which concerns the variable, is not science, nor, as action and production are different, is it art. It
is a reasoned state, capable of action in relation to things that
are good or bad for man. Thus, the term is applied to temperance. It is a virtue of that part of the soul that forms opinions,
because both it and opinion concern the variable.

vi *Intelligence or intuition (pp. 151–2)*

Scientific knowledge is forming judgements about universal
and necessary things, and depends on first principles. The
first principles of scientific truths cannot be grasped by science, art or prudence, for scientific truth is demonstrable, and
art and prudence are to do with the variable; nor are they the
sole concern of wisdom. If we reach the truth in relation to
variable and invariable things through art, science, prudence,
wisdom and intuition, and the one that apprehends first principles cannot be among the first three, it must be intuition.

vii *Wisdom (pp. 152–4)*

The term wisdom is used of the greatest experts in the arts.
But some are wise without qualification, so it is the most
complete form of knowledge. The wise man knows and understands the first principles and what follows from them, so

wisdom is intuition and scientific knowledge. It differs from
prudence, for even those animals that look after themselves
are thought prudent. It is not the same as political science,
for if people described what is beneficial to themselves as
wisdom, there would be more than one type. It is scientific
and intuitive knowledge of what is by nature most precious.
Prudence concerns human goods, about which there can be
deliberation, but nobody deliberates about things that cannot
be otherwise, and are not the means to an end (of a practical
good). One who excels in deliberation is able, by its means, to
aim at the best of the goods attainable by man. Further, prudence is about conduct, requiring knowledge of particular circumstances, rather than universals, and often those lacking
theoretical knowledge are more effective in action. Prudence
is practical, and needs both kinds of knowledge, but especially the former.

viii *The political sciences are species of prudence (pp. 154–7)*

Political science and prudence are the same state of mind.
Prudence concerning the state has two aspects: legislative and
political science, and the latter, dealing with particular circumstances, is practical and deliberative. Prudence especially
concerns the self, and it is to this that term itself is applied.
The other forms are domestic, legislative and political science.
Those who confine themselves to seeking their own good are
considered prudent, while politicians are seen as busybodies.
But it is impossible to secure one's own good independently
of domestic and political science. Young people may develop
ability in such fields as mathematics, but are not considered
prudent, which involves knowing particular facts, through
experience.

Detailed Summary of Aristotle's The Nicomachean Ethics

Prudence contrasted with science and intuition (pp. 156–7). Prudence is opposite to intuition: the second apprehends definitions, which cannot be logically demonstrated, while the first apprehends the ultimate particular, which cannot be apprehended by scientific knowledge.

ix Resourcefulness or good deliberation distinguished from other intellectual qualities (pp. 157–9)

Resourcefulness is a kind of deliberation, which is not knowledge, conjecture, readiness of mind or opinion. It is a type of correctness, as one who deliberates well does so correctly. It is correctness of thinking, and, as one who deliberates is enquiring into something, it is a species of correctness of deliberation. Correctness has more than one use. A wicked person can deliberate correctly to achieve something bad, but the result of correctness in deliberation (as in resourcefulness) is thought to be good. It is possible to achieve the right end by the wrong means, while someone may succeed after quick, as well as long, deliberation, all of which falls short of resourcefulness which is correctness in estimating advantage with respect to the right object, the right means and the right time.

x Understanding (pp. 159–60)

This differs from scientific knowledge or opinion, and is not a particular science. It does not concern eternal and immutable things, nor those that come into being, but matters that cause perplexity and require deliberation. It is in the same sphere as prudence, but the end of the latter is what one should or should not do, while understanding only makes judgements.

It is not having or acquiring prudence, but, in using the faculty of opinion, to judge another's account of matters within the scope of prudence, the act of judging rightly is called understanding.

xi Judgement and consideration (pp. 160–1)

This is the faculty of judging what is equitable correctly. It is commonly held that the equitable man is sympathetic in his judgements, and that it is sometimes equitable to do so. The latter is a correct judgement that decides what is equitable.

General comments on the various states of mind (pp. 160–1). We attribute judgement, understanding, prudence and so on to people indifferently. To be understanding and sympathetic is to be able to judge matters that concern the prudent man. Equitable acts are common to all good men in their behaviour towards others. A person may have judgement, understanding and intuition, but nobody is endowed by nature with wisdom. We should heed the opinions of older, experienced and prudent people, as their experience gives them insight.

xii The value of the intellectual virtues (pp. 162–3)

As to the use of the intellectual virtues, wisdom does not deal with things that make a man happy. Prudence concerns just acts that are good for man, but knowing about them does not enable us to do them. If prudence's use is to enable us to become good, this does not help those who are so already, and it could seem paradoxical that prudence, which is inferior to wisdom, has more authority. Wisdom and prudence are both virtues, each of one part of the soul, which are desirable in themselves. Wisdom produces happiness, as it is part of virtue

as a whole. Full performance of a human being's function depends on prudence and moral virtue together: the second ensures the correctness of our end, the former the means to it.
We must reconsider our view that prudence does not make us
any more capable of doing fine and just acts. We say that some
of those who perform just acts are still not just, but there appears to be a state of mind, in which someone can do things
in such a way as to be a good man. Virtue makes the choice
correct, but carrying out all the stages of action, to reach that
chosen end, is a matter for a different faculty.

A new factor: the faculty of cleverness (p. 164). The faculty
of cleverness can carry out actions that help to achieve our
proposed aim, and is praiseworthy if the aim is noble, but unscrupulous if it is not. It is implied by, but not identical with,
prudence, which the insight of the soul cannot reach without
virtue: one cannot be prudent without being good.

xiii How prudence is related to natural virtue and virtue proper (pp. 164–6)

Natural virtue's relation to true virtue is like that of prudence
to cleverness. Although it is generally believed that the various kinds of character are natural, we hold that moral qualities are actually acquired in another way, as natural dispositions tend to be harmful. It is when intelligence is acquired
that a person's conduct becomes outstanding, and his disposition is virtue in the full sense. It is this that implies prudence. Socrates and many others thought all the virtues are
forms of prudence, and, when virtue is defined, the qualification, in accordance with the right principle is added, which
accords with prudence: it is the right principle in moral conduct, and it is not possible to be good without prudence, or

prudent without moral goodness. Having the single virtue of prudence brings with it possession of them all. Correct choice cannot be made without goodness, which identifies the end, or prudence, which leads us to perform the acts that are the means towards it. But the latter does not have authority over wisdom, giving orders, not to it, but for its sake.

Book X

Pleasure and the Life of Happiness (pp. 254–84)

i The importance of pleasure in ethics, and the conflict of views about its value (pp. 254–5)

Pleasure is important in forming the character to like or dislike the right things, as people choose the pleasant and avoid pain. Some say pleasure is the good, others that it is wholly bad. Some of the latter really think this, but others, believing human beings are self-indulgent, think they need urging in the opposite direction, to attain the mean. But theories that are at odds with what our senses tell us can damage the cause of truth.

ii Eudoxus' view, that pleasure is the supreme good, is not above dispute (pp. 255–6)

As both rational and irrational creatures are attracted to it, Eudoxus thought that pleasure is the good; that, in every case, what is desirable is good; and that what is most desirable is best. All creatures being drawn to it shows it is best for all, as each individual seeks its own good; and what is good for all, which all try to obtain, is the good. He thought that people's shunning pain supported his view, holding that pleasure is desirable in itself, and what is never chosen as a means to something else is the most desirable thing. He also thought adding pleasure to something good makes it more desirable, but this suggests that pleasure is not the good, as any good thing is made more desirable by adding another to it. This was how Plato disproved the view that pleasure is the good, saying that intelligence makes the life of pleasure more desirable. Nothing can be the good, if it is made more desirable by adding something to it.

iii *The view that pleasure is not a good is also open to criticism (pp. 256–9)*

It cannot be argued that what both rational and irrational creatures try to obtain is not a good. Some say that good is determinate, but pleasure is indeterminate, as there are degrees of it, but this applies to justice and all other virtues. There are both pure and mixed pleasures, and there seems no reason why pleasure should not be determinate in the way health is, which has degrees. They assume that the good is perfect, that processes are incomplete, and that pleasure is the latter. But this seems wrong. Pleasure is said to be replenishment of our natural condition, but this is a bodily experience, so our bodies would feel the pleasure. This is not accepted, and arises from the pleasures of eating: it is thought that we experience a lack, and then find pleasure in replenishment.

Even the view that some pleasures are bad can be challenged (pp. 259–60). Those who say there are disreputable pleasures can be refuted by the argument that these are only pleasant to people of an unhealthy disposition, while others are not desirable, if obtained in the wrong way. Pleasures also differ in kind, and those arising from noble acts are not the same as those arising from base ones. No one would elect to have a child's mentality, even if this meant deriving the greatest pleasure from things children like, or enjoy a disgraceful activity, even if it had no bad consequences. Further, we wish to have many things, like memory and knowledge, even if they bring no pleasure. Pleasure seems not to be the good, as not every pleasure is desirable, and some pleasures, which are desirable in themselves, are superior in kind, or due to their sources.

iv Pleasure is not a process (pp. 260–2)

Pleasure, like seeing, seems to be complete at any moment. There is nothing the prolonging of which will enable its specific quality to be perfected. It is not a process, but is complete at any given moment. A movement must occupy time, whereas a feeling of pleasure does not.

The relation of pleasure to activity (pp. 262–3). Any sense's activity is at its best when the organ is in the best condition and directed towards the best of objects proper to it. Each sense has its corresponding pleasure, which perfects the activity, and this will occur, as long as the object of thought or sensation, and that which judges or contemplates, are in the right condition. The reason nobody feels pleasure continuously is probably fatigue, as no human faculty can be continuously active, and things please us when they are new, but then cease to do so.

Pleasure is essential to life (pp. 263–4). All are drawn to pleasure, directing their activities towards the objects, and through the faculties, they like best; pleasure perfects the former, and perfects life.

v As activities differ in kind, so do their pleasures (pp. 264–7)

Pleasures differ in kind: they intensify their activities; what intensifies something is proper to it; and things that are proper to things that are different are different themselves. The pleasures proper to serious and bad activities are respectively virtuous and vicious. Pleasures are as diverse as their activities, but intellectual ones are superior to sensuous ones, and both sorts differ among themselves. The proper pleasure of every animal is exercising its proper function. It would be reasonable to expect the pleasures of the same species to be the same, but the same set of things delight and annoy different groups of people.

Only the good man's pleasures are real and truly human (p. 267). The good man's view is the true one, so true pleasures will be the ones he enjoys, while those that displease him are not pleasures at all. Only investigation of human activities can show if there is one reputable pleasure that can be regarded as the pleasure of man.

vi Recapitulation: the nature of happiness (pp. 267–9)

Happiness is not a state, but relates to some activity. These are either chosen for themselves, or for the sake of something else, so we must class happiness as the former, as it needs nothing else. Such activities are those from which nothing is required beyond the exercise of the activity, which fits actions that accord with goodness.

Happiness must be distinguished from amusement (pp. 268–9). Pleasant amusements, not being a means to something else, are put in this class, but they lead people to neglect their bodies and property. However, as many, regarded as happy, including the powerful, engage in them, they are held to be conducive to happiness. But virtue and intelligence, the sources of serious activities, do not depend on being powerful. Such people may not have experienced refined pleasure, so there is no reason for regarding their preference as a worthy choice. It is what good people think valuable (virtuous activity) that really is such. It would be absurd to struggle through life, just to amuse ourselves.

Everything, except happiness, is chosen for something else's sake; the happy life is lived according to goodness, suggesting seriousness, not amusement. Human activity is more serious in proportion as it is better, so the activity of the better part is superior and more conducive to happiness. Anyone can enjoy bodily pleasures, but happiness is found, not in these, but in virtuous activities.

vii Happiness and contemplation (pp. 270–3)

This being so, perfect happiness is an activity that accords with the highest virtue, and which is more divine than any other part of us. This is contemplative activity, for the intellect is the highest thing in us, and apprehends the highest things that can be known. Happiness must contain pleasure, and those with knowledge pass their time more pleasantly than those pursuing it. Contemplation is also a self-sufficient activity. Just, brave and temperate people need others towards to whom they can be just, and so on, but the wise man can practise contemplation alone, and so is self-sufficient. Contemplation is also appreciated for its own sake, as nothing else is expected to be gained from it.

Since happiness is thought to imply leisure, it must be an intellectual, not a practical activity (pp. 271–2). Happiness is held to depend on leisure, but politics and war, in which the practical virtues are exercised, leave no room for it. Politics is about securing the happiness (one separate from politics) of the politician and his fellow-citizens. If politics and war, though noble and grand, are incompatible with leisure, and aimed at another end, whereas contemplation aims at no end beyond itself, and has a pleasure peculiar to itself, it will be man's perfect happiness, as long as he has a full lifespan.

Life on this plane is not too high for the divine element in human nature (pp. 272–3). One living such a life will do so through something divine in him, and, if the intellect is divine compared to man, intellectual life is divine, compared to human life. We must disregard those who say we should just think human thoughts, and instead live in keeping with the highest in us, which seems to be the true self of the individual. What is best and most pleasant for any creature is what is proper to it, and, for human beings, the pleasantest, and so the happiest life is that of the intellect.

viii Moral activity is secondary happiness (pp. 273–4)

A life conforming to the other kind of virtue will be happy in a secondary degree. Moral goodness is intimately connected with the feelings, and it and prudence are closely linked, as the moral virtues provide the first principles of prudence, while it sets the right standard for the virtues. The link between the moral virtues and the feelings means that the former belong to the composite person, so living in conformity with them, and its associated happiness, is human. Intellectual happiness is separate, but detailed treatment would go outside our present enquiry. It requires fewer external accessories than moral goodness, as the liberal man needs money to be liberal. It is not clear whether actions or intentions are more important in determining the goodness of conduct, but its perfection would require both, and, unlike contemplative activity, virtuous actions may require many accessories: but, as a human being and member of society, the individual chooses to act according to virtue, and needs external goods to do so.

The view that happiness is contemplation is confirmed by other arguments (pp. 274–6). Another argument for happiness being contemplative activity is that we think of the gods as supremely happy and blessed, but, if we listed actions like being brave, liberal or temperate, we would find the practical details unworthy of gods. As they are living and active beings, the only activity left is contemplation. So, among human activities, it is the most akin to that of the gods and it is the happiest. This is why the lower animals do not share in happiness: they are incapable of contemplation, while human life is happy, to the extent that it contains something resembling divine activity. The more people contemplate, the happier they are, but, being human, they also require external happiness, in the form of health and food. But happiness does not require many external goods: neither self-sufficiency nor moral conduct requires a superfluity of means, and private persons are thought to do more good acts than those in power. As Solon said, happy people have a moderate quantity of external goods, live temperate lives, and do the finest deeds. This needs to be tested against the facts of life. One using his intellect is likely to have the best state of mind, and to be loved by the gods, who take pleasure in the best part of human beings. They reward the wise man, so it is natural that he should be the happiest of men.

*ix So much for ethical theory. How can it be put into practice?
(pp. 277–84)*

It may be that the most important thing is not to outline happiness and the virtues, but to become good. Discourse may be
able to make an idealistic character susceptible of virtue, but it
will not impel the masses towards perfection. They are ruled
by fear, deterred from evil only by punishments, and have no
idea of the fine and pleasurable. It is impossible for any argument to overcome long-established habits, so we must be content if what is supposed to make us good enables us to attain
a degree of goodness.

*Goodness can only be induced in a suitably receptive charac-
ter (p. 278).* Views differ about whether people become good
by nature, habit or instruction. Nature is beyond our control,
while discussion and instruction do not always work. We need
a character which has affinity to virtue, and appreciates what
is noble.

*Education in goodness is best undertaken by the state (pp.
278–9).* Right training for goodness is hard to obtain, except
for those raised under right laws, so upbringing and activities
must be regulated by law. People respond to compulsion and
punishment better than argument, so legislators need to punish the disobedient, as well as appealing to the fine feelings of
those with habits shaped by decent training. To produce good
men, people require to be guided by the right system. But
most states completely neglect these matters.

*If neglected by the state, it can be supplied by the parent; but
it calls for some knowledge of legislative science (pp. 280–1).*
The individual must take on the role of legislator, if the state
does not, and help his children towards goodness. At home,
a father's instructions have the same weight as laws in the
state, are influenced by natural affection and, as there is indi-

vidual attention, are more accurate. The best instruction will be given by the instructor with general knowledge of what is good for all cases, and anyone wishing to have theoretical knowledge must study the universal. If people can be made good by laws, someone wishing to make other people better should acquire the art of legislation.

Where can such knowledge be obtained? Not from the sophists (pp. 281–3). As legislation is a branch of political science, the obvious people to learn it from would be politicians. But, unlike, say, medicine, the same people are not both practitioners and teachers: the sophists profess to teach political science, but politicians practise it on the basis of experience (a major contributor to political success), rather than reason. The sophists are ignorant of the subject, equating it with rhetoric, but laws are the products of the art of politics, so they cannot teach the art of legislation. Reading a handbook cannot equip someone to practise medicine, as it will only help the experienced. Similarly, collections of laws will only assist those with a formed habit of mind, who are able to judge what has been enacted rightly.

The student of ethics must therefore apply himself to politics (pp. 283–4). Legislation and constitutions should be studied closely, to make our philosophy of human conduct as complete as possible. We need to review valid statements made previously; decide, by looking at constitutions, the influences that conserve or destroy a state; and discover why some states, but not others, are well governed. This may enable us to determine the best kind of constitution and system of laws and customs.

Glossary

Academy (the). University, founded by Plato in the 380s BC, where the educational programme Plato sets out in his *The Republic* was followed, and which Aristotle attended.

Accepted beliefs. Traditional religious beliefs.

Agent. One who performs an action.

Alexander the Great. King Alexander II of Macedonia (356–323 BC). Son of Philip II, and one of the most successful generals in history, whose conquest of the Persian empire enabled him to extend the influence of Greek culture and civilization well beyond Greece itself.

Altruistic. Unselfish, putting the needs and well-being of others above one's own.

Anaxagoras. Greek philosopher and scientist, born in Ionia about 500 BC, who spent most of his life in Athens.

Another which is good in itself and the cause of whatever goodness there is in all these others. See forms below.

Appetitive part (of the soul). See desiderative part (of the soul) below.

Aquinas, Saint Thomas (1225–74). Italian-born philosopher, theologian and Dominican friar, whose setting forth of Roman Catholic teaching was declared definitive by Pope Leo XIII. His books include *Summa Theologica* (*Summa Theologiae*), the *Summa Contra Gentiles* and the *De Veritate*.

Argives did when they thought the Spartans were Sicyonians. This illustration is from the Battle of the Long Walls (the walls that protected the area between Athens and its port, the Piraeus) in 392 BC.

Art. Skill, in particular, human skill.

Athens. City-state in ancient Greece, which played a major part in defeating the Persian invasions of Greece, established a democratic system of government, and was famous as a seat of learning. The

Glossary

philosophers Socrates and Plato were Athenians, and Aristotle studied and taught there.

Boorishness. Ill-bred, uncouth behaviour.

Buffoonery. Foolish, waggish behaviour.

Calculative/contemplative parts of the intellect. Different parts of the intellect.

Categories (the). According to Aristotle, ten kinds of category or predicate could apply to the subject of a proposition/statement: substance, quality, quantity, relation, time, place, position, state, activity and passivity. In Book I, vi, Aristotle uses this theory to refute Plato's theory of the forms. See also universal(s) below.

Citizens. Those living in a Greek city-state, such as Athens.

Civic courage. Being willing to fight and face death for one's city.

Civic distinction. Honour(s) or admiration from/of fellow citizens.

Composite being. A human being, who consists of body and soul.

Contemplative (life). Intellectual activity, which brings happiness. See Book X, vii.

Continent/incontinent. Possessing or lacking self-restraint, particularly in relation to sexual desires.

Convention not nature. It is a matter of accepted practice that they are regarded as morally fine or just, not (necessarily) because of their intrinsic worth.

Deduction. Arguing from certain premises to conclusions from which they (may) follow necessarily.

Demonstrative state. One that can demonstrate, or prove conclusively, what is known.

Desiderative part (of the soul). The part of the soul concerned with desiring to perform an action. See also soul below.

Desire for its own sake. That which is desired for its own sake, not as a means to something else.

Determinate. That which is fixed or definite.

Determinism. The doctrine that every event has a cause. Applied to what are held to be voluntary human actions, it suggests that they are not really free. There are three main philosophical responses to this issue: 'soft' determinism, which argues that human freedom is compatible with determinism, and that human beings are free, unless subject to external constraint; 'hard' determinism, which holds that the causal connection between human motives and actions rules out genuine human freedom; and libertarianism, which maintains that the human will is free, and must be so if human beings are to be held responsible for their actions. Aristotle

Glossary

contends (Book III) that both virtue and vice are voluntary, because both good and bad people are equally free in their actions and their choice of means to their chosen ends, even if they are not free in their choice of ends.

Differentia. Distinguishing mark, that which identifies something as what it is.

Disposition(s). Inclination or tendency. Aristotle (Book II, v) defines it as the condition of being well- or ill-disposed towards something.

Efficient cause. The cause that produces the particular effect, and which makes a thing what it is.

Encomia. Expressions of high-flown praise.

End. That which is desired or aimed at.

Eternal. What has always existed, and will always exist.

Ethics. Study of what is good and right, of the difference between things that are good as ends or means, of the moral principles we should adopt and why.

Ethos. A Greek word, meaning custom or habit and also character.

Eudaimonia. The Greek word means 'happiness' or 'prosperity', which is the goal of ethics. Aristotle describes the happy man's way of life in Book X. It involves the exercise of the rational powers ('a virtuous activity of the soul', Book I, vii), and living well and successfully. It is a contemplative and active life (otherwise those who slept all the time might have it), and also a self-sufficient one: it stands in need of nothing else (it is not made more good by adding another good to it) and it is chosen for itself and not for the sake of something else.

Eudemus. Aristotle's pupil who edited *The Eudemian Ethics*.

Eudoxus (408–355 BC). Greek astronomer and mathematician, who studied under Plato.

Faculties. Generally, powers or abilities. Aristotle defines them (Book II, v) as abilities to have feelings. See feelings below and disposition(s) above.

Feelings. Desire, anger, fear and so on. See also faculties and disposition(s) above.

Final ends. Ends which are chosen/can only be chosen for their own sake and not for (or partly for) the sake of something else.

First principles. Those that are at the root of a particular investigation.

Forms (the theory of the). Plato held that the individual things in the ordinary, visible world, which we experience through our senses, acquire their identity by being (in some way) copies of

Glossary

the unchanging forms of these things in the intelligible world (which is discovered, known about, by the mind), to which only our minds give access. Thus, something is round by being a copy of, or participating in, the form of roundness. However, it will not be perfectly round, but will only approximate to roundness. This is a dualistic view of reality, as it holds that there are two orders or levels of reality and that universals (see below), such as roundness, exist independently of particular round things. Plato held that there is a form of the good (see good-itself below), and that only those who have seen it possess the highest form of knowledge; know what the good is in itself; and can say authoritatively what is good, right and just. Aristotle sets out his arguments against the theory of the forms in Book I, vi.

General happiness. The happiness of the majority/the greatest number of people. According to utilitarianism, right actions are those that maximize the happiness of the greatest number of people.

Gods. The Greek gods.

Good in themselves. Things that are intrinsically good, and which are pursued for their own sake, as opposed to things that are good as a means to something else.

Good-itself (the). Plato believed that there is a form of the good, which has the same relation to intelligible objects in the intelligible world as the sun has to visible ones in the visible world; which is the source of reality and truth; and which causes goodness in all things that are good.

Goods that are pursued or esteemed in their own right. Things that are good in themselves.

Happiness. This is the supreme good, or ultimate end, of human life. It is an end that is always chosen for its own sake and never as a means to anything else (Book I, vii). See eudaimonia above.

Hard determinism. See determinism above.

Hedonism/hedonisic. Selfish concern with promoting individual pleasure; the view that pleasure is the main or only thing that is good.

Heraclitus (c. 500 BC). Philosopher from Ephesus, who argued that things are in a state of flux and that matter is constantly changing.

Hermias. Ruler of Assos in Asia Minor, who was executed by the Persians. Aristotle married his niece, Pythia.

Honour. Reputation, good name: it is the goal of political life (Book I, v).

Induction. The most common form of reasoning, which infers probable conclusions from premises based on experience.

Glossary

Intelligible realm. See forms (the theory of the) above.

Intuition. Immediate mental awareness: the state of mind that apprehends first principles (Book VI, vi).

Irrational parts of the soul. The vegetative (see below) and desiderative (see above) parts.

Irony. Giving what is said additional force, by using words with a literal meaning that is the opposite of what is meant.

Libertarianism. See determinism above.

Licentiousness. Depravity, shameless immorality.

Lyceum. A grove and gymnasium near Athens, sacred to Apollo, where Aristotle taught.

Macedonia. Kingdom in northern Greece which in the fourth century BC became the dominant power in Greece under Philip of Macedonia and which under his son, Alexander the Great, defeated and conquered the Persian empire.

(Merely) useful. That which is (good as) a means to something else.

Mean (the doctrine of). The mid-point between the vices of excess and deficiency. Virtue is finding the mean between these two vices. See virtue below.

Moral virtues. See virtues below.

Nicomachus. Both Aristotle's father, court physician to King Amyntas II, and his son, the editor of *The Nicomachean Ethics*, were called Nicomachus.

Obsequiousness. Sycophancy, flattery.

Opinion. Belief based on conviction or probability, not proof.

Pericles (c. 500–429 BC). Athenian statesman, who developed Athenian democracy and dominated Athenian politics for the 30 years before his death.

Philip of Macedon, King Philip II of Macedonia (c. 382–336 BC). An able and successful military leader and father of Alexander the Great, who established Macedonian supremacy in Greece through a series of wars. He was assassinated in 336 BC.

Physical pleasure(s). Aristotle contrasts purely physical pleasures and refined or intellectual pleasures. The fact that many people, including those in positions of power, regard them as a source of happiness, does not make them a worthy choice, as such people may not have experienced more worthwhile pleasures.

Plato (c. 429–347 BC). Greek philosopher, who was a student of Socrates, and who taught Aristotle at his Academy (the world's first university) in Athens. His writings include *The Republic*, *Theaetetus*, *Symposium*, *Phaedrus* and *Laws*.

Glossary

Pleasure. That which gives enjoyment or satisfaction: ordinary people identify happiness with pleasure (Book I, iv).

Political science. Knowledge/study of how to govern a state, manage public affairs. Aristotle states that its main concern is to endow the state's citizens with such qualities as virtue and readiness to do fine deeds (Book I, ix).

Politics. How to govern, that which concerns governing, a state; managing public affairs.

Practical good. Good relating to action, rather than thought or speculation.

Priam. Legendary King of Troy at the time of the Trojan war, who was killed when the Greeks captured the city.

Prudence/practical wisdom. Generally, carefulness, good sense. Aristotle (Book VI, v) defines it as the ability to deliberate rightly about what is conducive to the good life generally.

Psychology. Here, the study of the soul.

Pure and mixed pleasures. Mixed pleasures are those which contain an element of pain.

Pusillanimity. Faint heartedness, mean-spiritedness.

Qua. As, in the capacity of.

Quality. One of the categories (see above), for example hard or green.

Rational principle. Reason, the ability to reason.

Refined pleasure(s). Intellectual pleasure(s), as opposed to purely physical ones.

Relation. One of the categories (see above), for example smaller or taller (than).

Rhetorician/rhetoric. One who has studied the theory of how to speak in public, one who practises oratory.

Right principle. The right principle in moral conduct is what accords with prudence (see above): it is not possible to be good without prudence, or prudent without moral goodness (Book VI, xiii).

Sanguineness. Excessive optimism about the prospects of being successful

Science. Systematic knowledge of a subject.

Sentient life. Having the ability to perceive things through the senses.

Single faculty. An activity or skill, of which a number of others are part.

Soft determinism. See determinism above.

Solon (c. 640–c. 558 BC). Athenian statesman, who reformed Athens' constitution and laws, and improved its economy.

Glossary

Sophists. Teachers of politics, rhetoric and mathematics, who were criticized by Socrates and Plato for putting too much emphasis on rhetoric, and the way things were expressed, rather than the substance of what was said.

Soul. Aristotle thought that the soul was associated with the body, was what enabled human beings to function, and made possible their intellectual and moral development. It consisted of rational and irrational parts (see below). For human beings, the good is an activity of the soul in accordance with virtue (Book I, vii).

Soul is part rational and part irrational. The soul consists of a rational part (the ability to reason) and irrational parts: the desiderative and vegetative.

Sparta. Greek city-state, which was governed by a hereditary military class. Its rivalry with Athens for supremacy in ancient Greece ended with Athens' defeat in the Peloponnesian War (431–404 BC).

Substance. One of the categories (see above). Substance is the essence of something, which makes it what it is, such as being a human being or cow.

Sum of goods. (Greater) total of good things.

Supreme good. That good, which is desired/chosen solely for its own sake. See happiness above.

Teleology/teleological view of the world. The view that everything in the world, including non-rational and inanimate things, has an end or purpose, determined by its nature which it does/ought to aim at.

Temperate/temperance. Moderate, abstemious.

The good. See supreme good above.

Transcendental realm. A world that is beyond or outside the empirical one. See forms (the theory of the) above.

Universal(s). A universal is a property or relation, such as roundness or goodness, of which there are particular instances, which thus have that property or relation in common. Plato (see forms, the theory of, above) held that universals exist independently of the particulars, but Aristotle maintained that they exist in them. See also categories (the) above.

Universal good. See good-itself (the), forms (the theory of) and universal(s) above.

Utilitarianism. A (consequentialist) moral theory which holds that acts are not right (or wrong) in themselves, but only to the extent that they promote pleasure/happiness and prevent pain.

Vegetative (part of the soul). That part of the soul concerned with nutrition and growth.

Glossary

Virtue. Generally, moral excellence, a positive character trait that makes someone morally good and admirable. For Aristotle, the virtues are human excellences. He divides them into two groups: the moral (those relating to a person's character) and the intellectual. He defines the former (Book II, vi) as a purposive disposition, lying in a mean between the vices of excess and deficiency. Individual moral virtues relate to specific spheres of action or feeling. Thus, in the sphere of fear and confidence, the virtue or mean is courage, while the vices are the excess of rashness and the deficiency of cowardice; in the sphere of pleasure and pain, the virtue or mean is temperance, and the vices the excess of licentiousness and the deficiency of insensibility (Book II, vii, viii). Moral virtues are acquired by habit. The mean does not apply to the intellectual virtues, such as wisdom, understanding and prudence, which are acquired through instruction (see Book VI).

Virtue ethics. Ethical system based on virtue(s), rather than an idea of what is good (at which we should aim) or right (what we ought to do), and which derives from *The Nicomachean Ethics*.

Wisdom (theoretical). The most complete or finished form of knowledge: the wise man knows and understands the first principles and what follows from them (Book VI, vii).